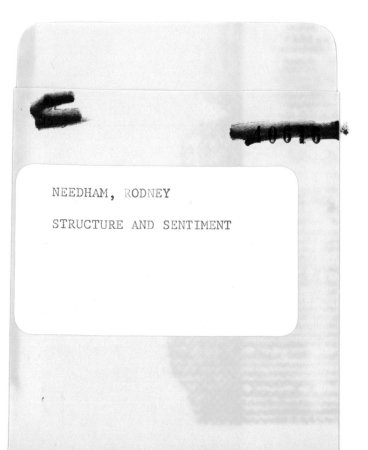

NEEDHAM, RODNEY

STRUCTURE AND SENTIMENT

STRUCTURE

AND

SENTIMENT

STRUCTURE

AND

SENTIMENT

A TEST CASE IN SOCIAL ANTHROPOLOGY

RODNEY NEEDHAM

The University of Chicago Press

CHICAGO & LONDON

Recipient of the Monograph Prize of the
American Academy of Arts and Sciences
for the year 1960
in the field of the social sciences

Library of Congress Catalog Card Number: 62-9738

THE UNIVERSITY OF CHICAGO PRESS, CHICAGO & LONDON
The University of Toronto Press, Toronto 5, Canada

To the Memory
of Marcel Mauss
(1872–1950)

PREFACE

This is a methodological essay, but it is pragmatic, not an empirically empty disquisition on how things ought to be done. I have written it in the conviction that the elaboration of method is best done in the resolution of particular problems; so I have taken an issue on which two very different theoretical approaches have been brought to bear, and I have tried to show that one is more useful than the other. The special methodological value of this test case lies in the fact that, exceptionally in social anthropology, it is a problem which, I think, can be quite definitely solved: of the two answers considered, one is essentially right and the other is demonstrably wrong.

There are two main reasons that I adopt this practical procedure. The first is that I wish the essay to constitute a protest against the vogue in unapplied methodology, programs for hypothetically superior research, evaluatory surveys of work done by others, introductions to social anthropology, conferences, and all such instruments and occasions for methodological pronouncements. It is a plea for getting on with the job, and this means for the most part making sense of particular things done by human beings in society. If one has anything useful to say, the thing to do is not to observe what a good idea it would be if something were done in a certain way, but to settle down to intensive work on the right class of facts and actually do it. The second reason is that whatever the value of textbooks and other such didactic means, they are appropriate only to masters of the subject who have demonstrated their personal competence in it; and by this I mean especially a record of having solved particular sociological problems, of having brought some kind of understanding where before there was puzzlement. So however just or weighty the methodological principles to which I adhere and which inspire this book, I should think it presumptuous that they be pronounced as general precepts by a junior and unknown academic. But by examining one problem I can, I think, show what it is that I advocate.

The issue that I deal with may be characterized as structural analysis versus psychological explanation, and it is a topic that seems to provoke heated reactions. I detest polemic, and I have tried to exclude any sign of aggressive controversy, but apparently I should add a further personal note. I am given to understand that what I have elsewhere written with the innocent desire simply to express an argument clearly and concisely, and above all to get things straight, has sometimes been taken as curt or contentious. I have to observe, therefore, that I have tried expressly to obviate this danger; but no man can properly appreciate his own style or tone, and I can only hope that no inappropriate note of asperity will obstruct the assessment of what to me appears a temperate argument.

The empirical substance of chapter 4 is abstracted from an article originally published in the *American Anthropologist,* and certain parts of chapter 5 first appeared in the *Southwestern Journal of Anthropology.* My thanks are due to the editors of these journals for permission to reproduce this material.

Much of the argument was worked out in lectures and classes at the University of Oxford in the years 1958–60. As presented here, it is virtually identical with the version submitted to the American Academy of Arts and Sciences in September, 1960. The subsequent changes amount to a number of minor expository alterations, and slight modification or development of the argument at a few points.

I wish to express to the American Academy of Arts and Sciences my gratification at the honor done me by the award of its Monograph Prize.

I am especially indebted and grateful to Professor Fred Eggan of the University of Chicago, who has most generously devoted much time to a critical and valuable examination of the manuscript and to making arrangements for its publication. Dr. E. R. Leach and Dr. T. O. Beidelman have also been so kind as to read it, and I offer them my thanks.

R. N.

Merton College, Oxford

CONTENTS

FIGURES

TABLES

INTRODUCTION

This book is about the possibility of explaining social institutions by reference to individual sentiments. In substance, it is a critique of *Marriage, Authority, and Final Causes: A Study of Unilateral Cross-Cousin Marriage*[1] by George C. Homans, a sociologist, and David M. Schneider, an anthropologist. Their monograph, which has many virtues, has been well received as "one of the most elegantly reasoned arguments ever to appear in anthropological literature" and as providing "a precise model in methodology which will be invaluable for teaching and for research on other problems." Its conclusions seem to have been generally accepted as correct and well established, and have even been incorporated in textbooks of elementary instruction.[2] I think, though, that its conclusions are fallacious, its method unsound, and the argument literally preposterous. In the following pages I try to show why.

Homans and Schneider's book is itself explicitly and almost exclusively an attack on Claude Lévi-Strauss's *Les Structures élémentaires de la Parenté*.[3] I have no brief to speak for Professor Lévi-Strauss, and I am uncertain to what extent he would endorse my views on the topic which has engaged our common interest; but I think his work should be defended, particularly against such a plausible and popular onslaught, and I hope he may agree that I am not entirely incompetent to do so. He has himself already written in its defense, but only extremely briefly, in a mere footnote.[4] His arguments are telling, but in such a

[1] Glencoe, Ill.: Free Press, 1955.

[2] Burling, 1960; Emmet, 1958, pp. 100–101; Freedman, 1957; Gluckman, 1956; Honigmann, 1959, p. 387; Mitchell, 1959, pp. 65–67; Slater, 1959, p. 1045.

[3] Paris: Presses Universitaires de France, 1949.

[4] Lévi-Strauss, 1958, pp. 344–45.

form they do not make the impression that they ought, and inevitably they leave much unsaid. For my part, I wish to defend it, in the first place, because I am convinced that *Les Structures élémentaires de la Parenté* is a masterpiece, a sociological classic of the first rank. It is the strength of this conviction which makes me go to these lengths on its behalf; and especially since those who have most approved Homans and Schneider's criticisms seem the least familiar with it. In the second place, there is a matter of scholarly principle. Lévi-Strauss's work is part of the continuing application, in the study of human society, of ideas and methodological rules worked out in the end of the last century and the beginning of this by the French sociological school. This school is the source of nearly everything that is best in social anthropology (to speak only of my own discipline); and if British social anthropology in particular has gained some renown, this is due largely to the "theoretical capital" left to it by French scholars such as Durkheim, Mauss, and Hertz. This inspiration continues in *Les Structures élémentaires de la Parenté*. On the other hand, there is a large and influential school of anthropology which for the most part has ignored, and continues as a matter of principle to ignore, the work and lessons of the French sociological school. In their place, it clings to certain attitudes and procedures which are not simply opposed to French sociological ideas (in reproaching it on this count I might merely be partisan) but have proved to be, on the whole, ineffective. That is, they have not in fact helped us to understand the phenomena which as social anthropologists we are trying to understand. *Marriage, Authority, and Final Causes* belongs to this tradition.

The institution with which both these books are concerned in common is unilateral cross-cousin marriage, and the problem is roughly this: Given that a society practices this form of marriage, why is it contracted with one side rather than the other? This may seem at first a narrow topic, but in comparing the arguments of the two books I am not making a simply technical appraisal of two rival explanations of a quite rare social phenomenon. I am attempting to contrast two radically different means of understanding social life; and to show that, in this instance at least, one is right and has helped us to understand something about human society, while the other is wrong and has not. That the particular institution examined is rare is of no importance in this context:

it is the generality of the methodological issues that counts, and the very rarity of the institution helps us in fact to arrive at a clear decision about them. As Homans and Schneider themselves remark, unilateral cross-cousin marriage is "a rare phenomenon that provides a crucial test of theory."[5]

There are two points to be made about the works compared in this inquiry. The first is that although I believe Les Structures élémentaires de la Parenté is a great book I do not by any means think it is perfect. There is much in it that I would dispute or recast on theoretical grounds, it suffers from serious lacks as regards sources, and it contains a number of ethnographic errors and misinterpretations of the facts. At times, too, Lévi-Strauss indulges in a figurative language to which writers in French seem particularly prone; and certain of these instances, taken in isolation, offer uncharacteristic grounds for the kind of charges that Homans and Schneider prefer. It would be pointless, though, to compile a catalogue of Lévi-Strauss's errors and weaknesses: the only useful and important course, which I shall pursue here, is to concentrate on those of his ideas which are interesting or profitable, and to see what more can be done with them. Yet the flaws are there, and in spite of the quality of Lévi-Strauss's insights it cannot be said that he has employed them to their proper effect in the analysis of any single system.

But these observations do not mean that I come anywhere near equating the scholarly value of Lévi-Strauss's work with that of Homans and Schneider's. There is first of all the difference of sheer scale between the two books: the former consists of 639 closely printed pages, comprising in large part minute analyses of societies covering a large area of the world; while the latter (64 pages) is hardly more than a longish article. Then there is the great difference in intellectual quality. In Lévi-Strauss's book, for all its real defects, there is a profusion of "analytical suggestions of the greatest brilliance."[6] On the other hand, Homans and Schneider's book is, in an exact sense, largely specious. As I shall try to show, it is defective in three prime and irremediable respects: (1) the authors have misunderstood and misrepresented Lévi-Strauss's views, and in so far as their argument relates directly to these it is wrong from beginning to end; (2) they have

[5] P. 3.   [6] Leach, 1951, p. 37.

3

preferred superficial statistical correlations in place of intensive analysis, forgetting that you cannot compare what you do not first understand; and (3) their analysis is fundamentally not sociological at all but psychological, and inapt to the solution of a sociological problem.

I do not assume that their views, jointly or severally, are still what they were when they wrote in 1955; but it is the book as printed, and as it continues to influence students, that I have to deal with. This brings me nevertheless to the dilemma which the critic of a joint work must face, even if there is little that he can do about it. *Marriage, Authority, and Final Causes* bears the names of two authors; but when one compares it with other things written by them individually, there appears to be a clear predominance on the part of Homans. I have this impression on grounds of both style and ideas, and so strongly that the book reads to me as though it could well have been written solely by him.[7] So although I have no alternative but to address my criticisms to the views expressed jointly by both authors, I should be less than frank if I concealed my conviction that Homans is not only the senior author but is the principal person with whose arguments I have to contend.

It should be appreciated that this little book is not intended to be a major work on prescriptive alliance. I have been working for some years on a theoretical monograph on the topic, making intensive comparative studies of a considerable number of societies, and when this is eventually published it will contain everything that I have to say on the matter. This, incidentally, is the chief reason that my critique has taken such a time to appear after the publication of the work it examines. The demands of teaching, field research, and other publications aside, it has cost an arduous and protracted effort to be quite sure of the facts about the societies in question; and not until I thought I had comprehended each particular case involved did I consider myself prepared to publish my own views. The present monograph is

[7] Cf. Homans, 1942, pp. 402–15; 1947; 1951; 1955; 1958. See in particular the quotations appended to my text. I should like however to register my admiration for Homans' *English Villagers of the Thirteenth Century* (1942), a work written while he was still professionally a historian and which in most respects (i.e., excluding the methodological conclusions in chap. 25) impresses me as an excellent piece of sociology.

limited severely to the aims I have outlined, and is designed to trespass as little as possible on the ground to be covered by the major inquiry. I draw on some of the material of the latter for the sake of illustration, and give some idea of the course of parts of its argument, but the two works are intended to be quite distinct. I regard *Marriage, Authority, and Final Causes* as important enough in its way to require refutation before I can proceed to the publication of intensive work on prescriptive alliance, and this is a task best performed separately. To examine it critically as I do here would take up too much of a study which should be more profitably occupied and more directly concerned with its topic, while the methodological issues are too large to be compressed into a small and introductory part of a comparative monograph. If therefore I deal sketchily with, or do not even mention, particular scholars or works or topics, it should not be assumed that they have necessarily evaded my attention or that I think them irrelevant. Similarly, my characterizations of certain societies are merely brief indications of features which are important in this context: they are based on minute analyses, but it should not be thought that they purport to be analyses in themselves.

I try constantly to be brief, though I am sorry to realize that I cannot attain the fresh brevity of Homans and Schneider's book. It is extremely difficult and frustrating to refrain from developing many engrossing points; but, if I did not, the result would be an extensive and different monograph, less suited to its purpose and less appropriate to the character of the work it examines. Still, I should like it to be kept in mind, even though my arguments may be thought conclusive enough as they stand, that there is much more to be said on each point; and, further, that although I try to deal comprehensively with Homans and Schneider's work I have not taken up every point that I consider incorrect or otherwise contributory to its invalidity.

It should be stressed that the ethnographic data on which I base my criticisms are taken practically exclusively from printed works, presumably available to Homans and Schneider and published well before the appearance of their monograph. It is true that in 1954–55 I did some work on asymmetric alliance on Sumba, but I mistakenly concentrated on comparative problems of structural change, and my researches exclusively into asymmetric alli-

5

ance really amount to little more than an extended reconnaissance. Also, at that time I did not see as clearly as I think I do now what the really important problems are, and I fear that many of my inquiries—however ethnographically informative—were for theoretical purposes misdirected. I do not, therefore, base my argument in any way on my field research. In any case, I should confine myself as a matter of principle to published sources, since in examining a current theory I think it right to use information which was accessible to its authors.

Finally, I hope no one will be deterred from tackling this essay by the extraordinary connotations which are sometimes attached to terms such as "cross-cousin." There is nothing very technical in it, the argument is quite simple, and it should offer something to anyone who shares my incredulity that "where a man finds love in one generation, he will find it in the next"[8] is really a sociological proposition.

[8] Homans and Schneider, 1955, p. 38.

Chapter One

> Interaction between persons is an exchange
> of goods, material or non-material. . . . This
> view has been much neglected by social
> scientists. So far as I know, the only theo-
> retical work that makes explicit use of it
> is Marcel Mauss's *Essai sur le Don,* which is
> ancient as social science goes.—HOMANS[1]

STRUCTURE

In this chapter the theme is introduced, the character of Lévi-Strauss's argument established, and the initial flaw in Homans and Schneider's exposed.

I

The theoretical theme derives from the genial observation of Marcel Mauss, in 1920, that exogamy is an *exchange* of women between clans.[2] In his *Essai sur le Don* he further made the point that prestations, among which he lists women, are exchanged by groups, not by individuals.[3]

This promising approach was taken up by the Leiden school of anthropology, which investigated empirically in a series of publications the way in which women, in certain Indonesian so-cieties, were exchanged in regular fashion between lineal descent groups. The particular system in which they were interested was that based on prescribed marriage with a matrilateral cross-cousin, a system to which they gave the name of "circulating connubium." The most notable of these investigations were pub-lished in the mid-thirties, but most of them were in Dutch and presumably for this reason went quite unnoticed by scholars out-side the Netherlands. In any case, they did not really take the theoretical application of the notion of "exchange" in this con-text very far, and it remained for another French scholar to un-dertake an intensive and comprehensive study of its implications.

[1] Homans, 1958, p. 598.

[2] Mauss, 1920, p. 396.

[3] Mauss, 1925, p. 36; 1954, p. 3.

This was Claude Lévi-Strauss, who in his *Les Structures élémentaires de la Parenté* (1949) for the first time formally isolated a certain type of exchange of women, defined the various modes in which it can be practiced and the kinds of groups between which women may be transferred, and postulated the several structural consequences of these rules.[4] Let us now look at certain centrally important features of his argument, and at Homans and Schneider's treatment of them.

II

The first concerns the type of marriage by which exchange-relationships are established; specifically, whether the rule of marriage is *preferential* or *prescriptive*. Whatever the structural entailments of any rules so distinguished, it has to be clearly recognized that by common usage in the English language (and in French) there is a great difference between them.

The term "preferential" implies that there is choice, and in the context of marriage that there is choice between a number of persons (distinguished genealogically, for example, or categorically) who may all be married. In this situation there may be a preference for one or more persons within the range of possibilities: for one reason or another, it is simply thought a good thing that a man should marry, if conveniently possible, a woman in a certain position. A very good study of this kind of situation is Schapera's paper on the marriage of near kin among the Tswana. To begin with, well over half of the marriages recorded for all social classes are with women who are not related at all, and preferences are thus exercised only in the minority of cases. "All Tswana . . . encourage marriage with first cousins. Preference is usually expressed for a cross-cousin, especially mother's brother's daughter. But father's brother's daughter is also favoured everywhere, and so is mother's sister's daughter except among Kwena and Ngwato. . . ." Marriages are actually recorded with a wide variety of relatives, viz., father's sister, father's brother's daughter,

[4] Cf. "Almost the only study I am aware of that begins to show in detail how a stable and differentiated social structure in a real-life group might arise out of a process of exchange between members . . . is Peter Blau's description of the behavior of sixteen agents in a federal law enforcement agency" (Homans, 1958, p. 604).

father's sister's daughter, mother's brother's daughter, mother's sister's daughter, brother's daughter, mother's sister, and sister's daughter. Within this range, preferences are exhibited which vary according to social class and generation: e.g., among the nobles the father's sister's daughter is clearly preferred to mother's brother's daughter, while among commoners the mother's brother's daughter is the most frequent choice.[5] The variety of possible spouses, and the variability in preferences, reflect a typical situation of choice.

The term "prescriptive," on the other hand, has quite different connotations. In this case the emphasis is on the very lack of choice: the category or type of person to be married is precisely determined, and this marriage is obligatory. Among the Batak of Sumatra, for instance, marriage is prescribed with a woman exclusively of the category *boru ni tulang,* of which one of the genealogical specifications is "mother's brother's daughter." Contrarily, a woman of the category of *boru ni namboru,* of which one of the specifications is "father's sister's daughter," may absolutely not be married.[6] This situation is characterized by an utter lack of categorical choice.

It is clear that these are formally two very different situations. In just what sociological respects they are different is a matter we shall look at shortly: the important thing at the moment is to realize that there is a radical distinction to be made. The question then is: to which type of marriage rule does Lévi-Strauss's argument apply? This needs to be gone into in some detail, for it is a point of quite crucial importance.

On the very first page of his text Lévi-Strauss says explicitly that his book is about systems which *prescribe* marriage with a certain type of relative (*les systèmes qui prescrivent le mariage avec un certain type de parents*).[7] It is by this feature that he defines an "elementary structure," which is distinguished from "complex structures," i.e., systems which leave the task of determining the spouse to other mechanisms, economic or social. (The Batak system is therefore an "elementary structure" while the Tswana is a "complex structure.") This is quite clear, but at certain points in the text there are ambiguities connected with the

[5] Schapera, 1957, pp. 140–41, 151–52.

[6] Keuning, 1948.   [7] Lévi-Strauss, 1949, p. ix.

use of the word "preferential." This word has commonly been used in anthropological literature to designate both prescriptive and non-prescriptive rules of marriage; and unfortunately Lévi-Strauss, adopting it from his sources and from current usage, himself uses it on occasion to designate marriages which are in fact prescribed. It is also the case, conversely, that in certain ethnographic instances he deals with marriage preferences as though they were prescriptions. Confusions of this sort have made it possible to maintain, though not with any plausibility, that Lévi-Strauss's argument in *Les Structures élémentaires de la Parenté* applies to marriage preferences; and it has to be shown that this cannot be the case.

Let us first look at certain passages occurring throughout the book. "Preferential union" is defined as "the obligation to marry within a group. . . ."[8] This illustrates both my points: that Lévi-Strauss is concerned with obligatory rules of marriage, and that he may confusingly refer to them as "preferential." On the other hand, sociologists are reproached with having failed to show the singular importance of cross-cousin marriage, by subsuming it with other rules such as the levirate, sororate, and avuncular marriage under the rubric of "preferential": "these latter are not preferential unions, because they cannot, in any group, constitute the exclusive or even preponderant rule of marriage; we would rather term them privileged unions (*unions privilégiées*), since they presuppose other modes of marriage, on to which they themselves are grafted."[9] One may regret Lévi-Strauss's use of "preferential," but this passage shows without possibility of doubt that he is dealing with "exclusive," i.e., prescriptive, rules of marriage. In discussing the Kachin system, moreover, he writes exactly that "the type of potential spouse is prescribed."[10] Further, he writes that in matrilateral cross-cousin marriage the father's sister's daughter is "excluded,"[11] which shows that the system is not defined by preference but by prescription. As a final quotation we may take the definition of "complex structures" as being those without a "positive determination of the type of preferred spouse."[12] Here Lévi-Strauss persists in the unfortunate use of the word "preferred," but the expression "positive determination"

<hr/>

[8] P. 56.

[9] P. 154.

[10] P. 313.

[11] P. 547.

[12] P. 575.

clearly excludes Tswana-like situations of preference and shows once again that he is concerned with prescriptions.

Such textual points could be multiplied, but there is another indication of the purport of Lévi-Strauss's argument that we should turn to. This is the fact that the societies to which he devotes the major part of his analytical survey—Australian aborigines, Kachin, Gilyak—undeniably practice prescriptive marriage; and that in his more speculative reconstructions of earlier marriage systems in India and China he clearly seeks to prove the earlier existence of prescriptive marriage there. The former societies are presented as examples of "elementary structures"; while the term "complex structures" is applied to forms of marriage in Africa, where prescriptive systems are very rare, and in Europe, where they are totally absent.

It is true that Lévi-Strauss claims incidentally that exchange is the universal form of marriage;[13] and that elsewhere, in some comments on the passage from elementary to complex structure, he envisages the possibility of the notion of "exchange" being usefully applicable in the analysis of non–prescriptive marriage also. But these observations cannot controvert the tenor of his explicit definitions, or the significance of the analyses which he actually carries out. In *Les Structures élémentaires de la Parenté*, Lévi-Strauss is concerned to analyze prescriptive rules of marriage, not preferential.

Now what do Homans and Schneider take Lévi-Strauss to mean, and what is their own theory about? The answer is, in the first place, *preferential* marriage. They write of Lévi-Strauss's book that it is "not a study of kinship behavior in general but of preferential marriage,"[14] and what they mean by "preferential" may be shown by a few quotations. "Preferential marriage is the familiar fact that in many societies ego, besides being forbidden to marry certain women, is expected to marry one or more of a class of women standing in certain kin relationships to him."[15] Note especially the word "expected" (i.e., not "enjoined" or "obliged") and the plural "relationships." Again, unilateral cross-cousin marriage is said to exist "when, as between the two kinds

13 Pp. 292, 593.

14 Homans and Schneider, 1955, p. 3.

15 P. 3.

of female cross-cousin—mother's brother's daughter and father's sister's daughter—the members of the society say that they prefer or expect ego to marry one of the two, but disapprove or at best tolerate his marriage with the other."[16]

But their position is ambiguous, as is shown in the first place by the opening words of their special hypothesis, to which they must be presumed to have given special thought: "Societies in which marriage is allowed or preferred with mother's brother's daughter but forbidden or disapproved with father's sister's daughter. . . ."[17] This passage proves that in fact they do not distinguish between preference and prescription, for rules of both types are covered (even if imprecisely) by the hypothesis. Moreover, they include in their test cases (which we shall examine in chapter 3) a number of societies in which unilateral cross-cousin marriage is actually prescribed. On balance, however, it is clear from their own words and formulations that they are concerned in the first place with preferences, not prescriptions. It is true that they write at two points of a rule "prescribing" marriage, and at another of men of a certain lineage "always" marrying women of another, thus implying a prescriptive rule of marriage.[18] But there is no doubt that they imagine Lévi-Strauss's theories to apply to "preferences"; and that their own, though applied incidentally to prescriptions also, is specifically intended to do so.

III

The next point to clear up is the determination of the person with whom marriage is prescribed. Lévi-Strauss's theory deals with cross-cousin marriage, and there are three types of cross-cousin, viz., bilateral, matrilateral, and patrilateral. Homans and Schneider's book is concerned only with the latter two. Now when Lévi-Strauss refers to these types of "cousin" what does he mean? Is marriage prescribed with the individual daughter of the mother's uterine brother, for example, or with a member of a more extensive class?

The clear answer is that his theory of exchange does not refer to genealogically defined individuals. When he writes of marriage with the "mother's brother's daughter" he does not mean

[16] P. 5.   [17] P. 28.   [18] Pp. 4, 12.

solely the individual first cousin, but a member of a class otherwise defined which merely includes this individual. He writes, for instance, that the class of marriageable cross-cousins is determined simply by eliminating the class that is forbidden, and that the best proof of this is that there is no trouble if a potential spouse of the required degree of cousinage is lacking, for a more distant relative is substituted.[19] The correctness of the phrasing is a matter for examination, but at least it emerges from the page cited that Lévi-Strauss is referring to a class of relatives and not to an individual: if a first cousin is lacking, any other "cousin" of the same category—whatever her degree of relationship—will do. As he makes clear in a remark on bilateral cross-cousin marriage, "the terms must be understood in a classificatory sense."[20] Also, with regard specifically to marriage with the matrilateral cross-cousin, we are told that it represents the systematic application, "to all degrees of kinship," of the formal alternation of sex on which the existence of cross-cousins depends.[21]

This feature in Lévi-Strauss's analyses becomes even clearer when we deal also with a related question, viz., between whom is alliance established by these prescribed marriages? Is it, for example, between the two families of a brother and a sister, or is it between two larger and corporate groups? Let us turn for illustration to Lévi-Strauss's major analysis of matrilateral cross-cousin marriage, that devoted to the Kachin. In this he writes that "the preferred marriage results, not so much from a prescribed and precise degree of relationship, but from a general relationship between all the men of a lineage . . . and [another] lineage in respect of all of its daughters and sisters."[22] The relationship is established or perpetuated "between groups rather than individuals,"[23] and the prestations associated with this type of marriage are made "between groups, not between individuals."[24] Again, in another society, what is taken to be the same type of marriage "results from a relation between lineages rather than from a prescribed degree between individuals."[25] Finally, in examining a matrilateral system among the Gilyak, he writes that "clans" are related by prescribed marriage, and that it is

[19] Lévi-Strauss, 1949, p. 60.

[20] P. 525. [22] Pp. 297-98. [24] P. 315.

[21] P. 552. [23] P. 312. [25] P. 333.

enough for one woman to marry into another clan for all the women of the latter to be forbidden to the men of her natal clan.[26] There is thus no doubt possible that these alliances through prescribed marriage are established between corporate groups, specifically lineal descent groups, not merely between individuals, and not between individuals standing in any particular genealogical relationship.

Once again, what do Homans and Schneider take Lévi-Strauss to mean, and what is their own theory about? First the question of what is meant by "cross-cousin." On this they are admirably exact and unambiguous. Their hypothesis, they say, "deals with the immediate cross-cousins and has nothing to say about more distant ones, such as mother's mother's brother's daughter's daughter."[27] "We have chosen to consider only the immediate cross-cousins and not more distant ones."[28] Furthermore, they write that if "the ideal system cannot be carried out, . . . the men will marry classificatory cross-cousins": that is, they think that as a matter of fact the cousin concerned in the societies under consideration is indeed the first cousin, and that not to marry her is to "depart from the norm."[29]

On the second point they are less clear, but the general burden of their argument has to do with "interpersonal relations," and they admit that they may be charged with putting their argument in terms of "the motives and behavior of individuals" instead of following Lévi-Strauss's emphasis, as they understand it, on "norms."[30] They are concerned to show how interpersonal relationships are "determined" and how these determine "marriage preferences."[31] Thus, although they are interested in the sociological feature of linearity as a determinative factor, they are really concerned with the relations between individuals, not with corporate groups.

IV

The next point has to do with the solidary consequences of matrilateral and of patrilateral cross-cousin marriage. Compare the systems diagrammed in Figures 1 and 2. They are both based, conventionally, on patrilineal descent. Figure 1 represents the

---

[26] Pp. 362–63.

[27] Homans and Schneider, 1955, p. 28.

[28] P. 32.

[29] P. 6.

[30] P. 25.

[31] P. 36.

formal features of prescribed matrilateral cross-cousin marriage; Figure 2, patrilateral.

The central fact in a matrilateral system is that lines are related by the same kind of relation from instance to instance and from generation to generation. Viewed as a system for the communication, transfer, or "exchange" of women, all the transactions are made in the same "direction." Three lines satisfy the structural

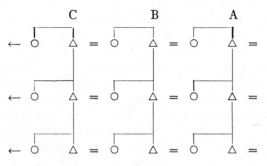

Fig. 1.—Matrilateral system

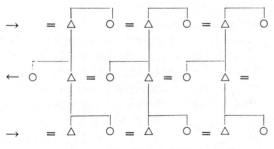

Fig. 2.—Patrilateral system

requirements of such a system, and the model entails that the movement of women is cyclic. Line A gives women to B, B gives to C, and C in turn gives to A, thus closing a cycle. Lévi-Strauss has expressed himself in rather different senses about the use of this notion of "cycle" in analyzing the actual operation of such an alliance system, but this is his fundamental conception of the defining features of the system. There are two points to be made about this model. First, it confirms that Lévi-Strauss's argument applies only to a prescriptive rule of marriage; for if the practice were merely preferential there could be no communication of women exclusively in one direction, there could be no clear and continuing distinction between wife-giving and wife-taking lines, and a social system of this kind could not result. The second point is that by adopting it in their own work Homans and Schneider assert by its implications also the applicability of their theory to prescriptive alliance; and they thus commit themselves, moreover, to arguing about preferences in terms appropriate only to prescriptive systems.

Lévi-Strauss calls this mode of transfer of women "generalized exchange" or "indirect exchange." It may seem a little odd at first that the word "exchange" should be applied to a system in which direct reciprocal interchange between two lines is by definition impossible, but it can easily be seen how the notion is to be understood. Line B, for example, gives its women to line C and cannot take women from C, but it must get women from somewhere, viz., from A. Women whom it gives away to one side are replaced by women from the other. Women are thus indirectly "exchanged" for women, and it is the rule of marriage which insures that women ceded will be replaced. (They are also as a matter of fact exchanged directly for other prestations, but the term "generalized exchange" denotes in the first place systems of exchanging women.)

With a patrilateral prescription, on the other hand, the situation is quite different (Fig. 2). As can readily be seen from the diagram, the direction in which women are transferred is reversed with each generation. This results in what Lévi-Strauss calls a "closed system" in which a cycle of exchange between any two lines is opened and closed in the following manner: a woman is ceded in one generation, another is acquired in the next (thus replacing the first), and the system "returns to a point of inertia." This form of marriage, Lévi-Strauss maintains, is only capable of forming a multitude of small closed systems of this sort, juxtaposed one to the other, without ever being able[32] to attain an

---

[32] This expression leads me to remark that Homans and Schneider's translations from the French do not always show the minute care for literal exactitude that one could wish. They translate this passage, for instance, as "without ever realizing" (p. 12), but the French is *sans jamais pouvoir réaliser* (Lévi-Strauss, 1949, p. 553). That is, Lévi-Strauss is speaking of an ineluctable structural feature, whereas their translation permits the inference that he may to some extent have in mind a contingent matter of fact. A tiny point, which the context should correct, but a trifle disturbing when so much hangs on a precise comprehension of the text.

over-all systematic character. The most to be expected with patrilateral marriage is a "collective harmony" resulting in a mechanical and precarious way from the sum of the particular ties by which a family links itself sometimes to one family, sometimes to another. This kind of reciprocity-structure belongs to a type which brings with it a "perpetual disequilibrium." Lévi-Strauss concludes that patrilateral cross-cousin marriage is "not a system but a procedure," and that there is no law or formula which can cover its operation. Since it has no systematic character and does not produce an organic type of solidarity, a society based upon it is always in a precarious position.

It is for this reason, says Lévi-Strauss, that matrilateral cross-cousin marriage is far more frequent than patrilateral: "If, then, in the final analysis, marriage with the father's sister's daughter is less frequent than that with the mother's brother's daughter, it is because the second not only permits but favors a better integration of the group, while the first never succeeds in creating anything but a precarious edifice made up of juxtaposed materials, subject to no general plan, and its discrete texture is exposed to the same fragility as that of each of the little local structures of which ultimately it is composed."[33]

This is the contention against which Homans and Schneider have written their book, and it is important therefore to examine further just what Lévi-Strauss is asserting and what they represent him as saying. The key expression is "a better integration" (*une meilleure intégration*). Homans and Schneider construe this as meaning that the matrilateral is more common than the patrilateral rule simply *"because it is better* for society,"[34] the emphasis being on the word "better." In this they are gravely misleading. Lévi-Strauss's argument is about integration, not simply about what is generally "better" for society. This is shown in another phrasing by Lévi-Strauss of the same assertion about the solidary consequences of the matrilateral rule, viz., that it permits "a greater organic solidarity" (*une plus grande solidarité organique*).[35] There is only one other place in the book where he himself uses the word "better" in this connection. This is where he

[33] Lévi-Strauss, 1949, p. 558. Cf. Homans and Schneider's translation (1955, p. 13), which in three particulars, though admittedly none is of grave consequence, is inexact.

[34] P. 13; their italics.

[35] Lévi-Strauss, 1949, p. 548.

17

contrasts the two forms of unilateral cross-cousin marriage and observes that the matrilateral presents "a 'better structure' than" the patrilateral. But note that it is he himself who puts the words "better structure" in quotation marks; and he emphasizes that this superiority is purely formal, and that his analysis in this respect is devoid of explanatory value.[36]

These are the only two places in his 639 pages where Lévi-Strauss uses the word "better" in connection with matrilateral cross-cousin marriage. It is highly curious, therefore, to observe that in their little book Homans and Schneider, in attacking Lévi-Strauss's argument about solidarity or integration as an explanatory notion, use the word "better" twenty-four times,[37] the word "good" eleven times,[38] and the word "goodness" three times,[39] a combined total of thirty-eight uses of these words. One can only wonder why they ever chose to characterize Lévi-Strauss's argument by such morally evaluative terms, so insistently and deceptively framing the issue in an idiom quite foreign to his structural concern with solidarity and integration.[40]

These latter terms themselves are of course difficult and imprecise, but they make sense, and are indeed fundamental to sociological understanding. We do commonly and usefully write of degrees of integration, and of the different solidary effects of certain institutions, and it would be difficult to imagine sociological inquiries which made no reference to these aspects of social relations. In particular, it certainly makes sense to inquire whether there is any difference in the solidary consequences of the two contrasted forms of unilateral cross-cousin marriage. Formally, as modes of exchange, they are certainly very different. Are these systematic differences of any effect in the organization of social life? This is Lévi-Strauss's central concern in contrasting the two rules, and whether or not one concurs with his characterization

[36] Pp. 551–52.

[37] Pp. 9, 12, 13, 14, 15, 16, 17, 18, 19, 20, 29, 58, 59, 60.

[38] Pp. 13, 16, 17, 18, 19, 20, 35, 39.

[39] Pp. 31, 34, 36. Cf. also "admires" (p. 6) and "bad" (p. 31).

[40] One consequence, at any rate, has been to mislead at least one reviewer and probably his readers into accepting it as "Lévi-Strauss's view that this form of preferential marriage [viz., matrilateral] is somehow better for society as a whole" (Freedman, 1957, p. 285).

of the systems featuring them, it remains a central and inescapable problem. Yet Homans and Schneider fail to see this as a problem, and explicitly decline to consider it in the formulation of their own theory. In any case, they seem not to understand Lévi-Strauss's conception of "organic solidarity" with regard to marriage. "For Lévi-Strauss the greater the marriage specialization of each of the kin-groups in a society, the greater the dependence of each upon all, and hence the greater the organic solidarity."[41] Specialization is indeed an issue, as is illustrated in the passage where Lévi-Strauss characterizes the relation between brothers as mechanical solidarity, and that between brothers-in-law as organic solidarity.[42] But it is the type of systematic relation and the solidary effects produced that are important, not the preponderant degree of any characteristic such as mere intricacy. For example, a bilineal section-system entails a greater specialization of groups connected by marriage than a matrilateral system, but it does not thereby possess a greater organic solidarity; and in fact the burden of part of Lévi-Strauss's argument is that such a section-system is incapable of attaining the general solidarity secured by the latter. If Homans and Schneider's statement were correct, the more intricate a marriage system the greater the organic solidarity; but neither in fact nor in Lévi-Strauss's argument is this the case.

V

Finally, there is the point concerning linearity. This can be dealt with very briefly, but it is nonetheless important and is the point at issue in one of the two main criticisms leveled against Lévi-Strauss by Homans and Schneider.

Lévi-Strauss at one point considers matrilateral cross-cousin marriage in matrilineal societies as well as in patrilineal, and he comes to the following conclusion: "It can be clearly seen therefore that the structure of generalized exchange does not depend at all on descent, but solely on the harmonic character of the regime considered."[43] By "harmonic" he means a society which is

[41] Homans and Schneider, 1955, p. 10.

[42] Lévi-Strauss, 1949, p. 599.

[43] P. 334.

patrilineal and patrilocal, or matrilineal and matrilocal, i.e., one in which the rule of descent and the rule of marital residence are of the same character. It is possible to argue about the precision of these criteria and about the validity of the proposition, and it is certainly the case that the two societies which Lévi-Strauss cites in support of it do not in fact practice prescriptive marriage and are therefore not strictly relevant to his announced topic of study. But the proposition is there and it is significant, and Homans and Schneider make it the focus of an important part of their argument.

What exactly is Lévi-Strauss saying? The essential thing to be appreciated is that he is concerned with structural possibility. He is saying that matrilateral cross-cousin marriage is possible in either a patrilineal or a matrilineal society, so long as the system is harmonic. He is not concerned with, and says nothing about, statistical frequencies. If it were the case that all societies practicing generalized exchange were patrilineal and patrilocal except one, and that the one were matrilineal and matrilocal, then his proposition would be validated. Even if no such society existed, the proposition would still hold in a formal sense: matrilineal and matrilocal societies exist and form viable systems, and there is no obvious structural reason to deny or doubt that such a society might also practice prescriptive matrilateral cross-cousin marriage.

The actual statistical occurrence of such societies is of course interesting, and the place of linearity in prescriptive marriage systems is clearly of general importance; but these are matters outside the scope of Lévi-Strauss's proposition. Note particularly his use of the word "depend" (*ne dépend nullement de*). This word, in its Oxford definitions, means among other things to be contingent on, or conditioned by; to rest entirely upon for support.[44] It has the same connotations in French, with the particularly significant meaning of "to be the consequence of," as in *l'effet dépend de la cause*.[45] So Lévi-Strauss is saying that matrilateral alliance is not dependent on the rule of descent, that its structural feasibility is not contingent upon whether the descent system is patrilineal or whether it is matrilineal. That is, there is

[44] *Shorter Oxford English Dictionary, s.v.* "depend."
[45] *Nouveau Petit Larousse,* 1952, *s.v.* "dépendre."

20

no necessary connection between line of descent and laterality of prescription. I would stress that these are not niggling or sophistical points of literal detail: we have to be absolutely clear about what Lévi-Strauss actually says before we can appreciate Homans and Schneider's criticisms or assess the value of their own contrasted and purportedly sounder views.

Now let us look at Homans and Schneider's understanding of the issue. "What we do reject is the claim that matrilateral cross-cousin marriage has nothing to do with linearity; we predict, Lévi-Strauss to the contrary, that it will tend to occur in patrilineal societies."[46] This is not just a local infelicity of expression, for they repeat their words exactly in their concluding retrospect of the argument, where they render one of Lévi-Strauss's "two crucial statements" as: "the adoption of the matrilateral form [of marriage] . . . has nothing to do with the linearity of a society."[47]

In these two places they diverge in three critical respects from Lévi-Strauss. First, he nowhere says or implies that linearity has "nothing to do"[48] with the rule of marriage, i.e., that there is no relation at all between rule of descent and rule of marriage. What he is saying, as we have seen, is that there is no necessary connection between them—a quite different matter. Second, his proposition neither affirms nor denies any statistical correlation such as that the matrilateral rule "tends to occur" in patrilineal societies. Given his statement of structural feasibility, the matter of the differential association of the rules in question is an entirely separate issue of a factual kind.[49] Last, attention should be drawn to the artificiality of the notion of a society "adopting," as Homans and Schneider put it, one rule of marriage or the other. Lévi-Strauss certainly does not argue in this fashion; and it introduces considerations of history, conscious assessment, and deliberate decision which (as we shall see) are quite foreign to the structural factors which are his concern.

[46] Homans and Schneider, 1955, p. 30.

[47] P. 56.

[48] It may be, of course, that the authors have simply misconstrued the French, though I should think this unlikely.

[49] See Lowie (1956), who appears to have been misled by the argument of the book he was reviewing into writing that: "In opposition to Lévi-Strauss, the authors hold that unilinear [*sic*] cross-cousin marriages are correlated with linearity. . . ."

VI

Homans and Schneider proclaim their "desire to meet Lévi-Strauss so far as possible on his own ground,"[50] and this is indeed a precondition of valid criticism or useful theoretical discussion. But they have instead misunderstood and consequently misrepresented what Lévi-Strauss has written,[51] and their own theory—whether right or wrong—is thus largely irrelevant to his.

Whereas his theory relates to prescriptions, theirs is concerned primarily with mere preferences; whereas he is concerned with marriages to women of any genealogical degree within particular categories, they restrict themselves exclusively to marriages between first cousins; whereas he deals with alliances between corporate descent groups, they consider only particular marriages between individuals; whereas he deals with the different solidary consequences of different rules of marriage, they ignore this issue and instead misrepresent him as being in some way morally concerned with the effects of such rules; and whereas he writes of the structural compossibility of rules of descent and rules of marriage, they misrender his proposition as maintaining that there is no relation between them.

In these five fundamental respects, then, there is almost no connection between Lévi-Strauss's views and Homans and Schneider's criticisms. It is on the basis of this aggregation of misconceptions that they claim to be "playing Darwin to his Lamarck."[52]

[50] P. 33.

[51] Contrast: "The authors demonstrate . . . that Professor Lévi-Strauss's theory is unsatisfactorily formulated . . ." (Gluckman, 1956).

[52] Homans and Schneider, 1955, p. 18. Cf. "Lévi-Strauss's book is magnificent in almost every respect save its major argument" (Homans, 1955, p. 137).

Chapter Two

> In discussing the element of sentiment we
> are on dangerous ground.—HOMANS[1]

SENTIMENT

*The structural issue having been posed, the opening arguments
against Homans and Schneider's psychological explanation can
now be deployed.*

I

Homans and Schneider's chief methodological concern is the
distinction between final cause and efficient cause in sociological
explanation. They characterize Lévi-Strauss's as a final-cause theory, and they present their understanding of his position in the
following words: "An institution is what it is because it is good
for society in the sense of creating organic solidarity, and some
institutions are, from this point of view, better than others."[2]
But, they argue, a final-cause theory is not good enough: "To
account for the adoption by a society of a particular institution,
it is, in principle, never sufficient to show that the institution is
in some sense good for society."[3] What is needed is an efficient
cause, and they ask what this is in Lévi-Strauss's scheme. Since
he does not explicitly speak of efficient causes, they are reduced
to the conjecture that in his view "members of some societies
chose matrilateral cross-cousin marriage because they could 'see,'
in much the same way that Lévi-Strauss himself can 'see,' that it
was better than other forms."[4] In other words, "Lévi-Strauss's

[1] Homans, 1942, p. 406.

[2] Homans and Schneider, 1955, p. 16.

[3] P. 17.

[4] P. 19. See also: "The argument [i.e., Lévi-Strauss's] assumes that primitive people not only 'see' what is good for their tribe—organic solidarity—
and want it for themselves, but also are able to attain the good, even when
this means giving up short-run personal interests for long-run social ones"
(Homans, 1955, p. 136).

efficient cause is human intelligence."[5] But, they reasonably proceed, it is bitterly difficult to persuade men to risk their individual short-term interests in favor of eventual benefits to society; and it is doubtful whether the intelligent recognition of what would be good for society is ever a sufficient condition for its adoption.

This is an obvious enough consideration, and it prompts one to ask whether Homans and Schneider have correctly characterized the theory of Lévi-Strauss with which their own is to be contrasted. Is it really a final-cause theory?

Perhaps it will be as well at this point to set down what is commonly understood by the terms "final cause" and "efficient cause." A final cause is "the purpose or end of the thing caused" (*S.O.E.D.*); "le but en vue duquel s'accomplit un acte" (Lalande). An efficient cause is "the producing agency" (*S.O.E.D.*); "le phénomène qui en produit un autre . . . ou quelquefois l'être qui produit une action" (Lalande).

One would immediately suppose that any theory advanced by Lévi-Strauss would be unlikely in the extreme to be of the sort ascribed to him by Homans and Schneider. He is, after all, a French anthropologist, carrying on a tradition directly derived from the early *Année Sociologique* school, to which he has clearly declared his allegiance; and it is well known that Durkheim explicitly rejected this kind of argument in sociological explanation: "To show how a fact is useful is not to explain how it originated or why it is what it is."[6] In fact, Lévi-Strauss does not try to account for the origin or "adoption" of any particular marriage rule, and he does not try to explain the simple existence of any marital institution by reference to its utility.

Nor does he anywhere in his book speak of purposes or ends in relation to unilateral cross-cousin marriage, or of members of societies choosing one or another rule with any particular resultant benefits in mind. When, for example, he discusses the ways in which members of simple societies analyze or describe their own social systems, and how they may teach or acquire theoretical representations of different systems, his object is not to claim that they thus make choices of "better" institutions: it is to show that the validity of a structural approach is confirmed by the people's

[5] Homans and Schneider, 1955, p. 19.

[6] Durkheim, 1901, p. 111.

own apprehension of the structures posited by the anthropologist.[7] The pages that Homans and Schneider refer to, in which Lévi-Strauss contrasts the solidary consequences of matrilateral and patrilateral cross-cousin marriage,[8] do not permit the interpretation which they put upon them, viz., that members of some societies are thought to choose matrilateral marriage because they can "see" its social advantages.[9] And certainly the quotation by Lévi-Strauss of proverbs from societies following the matrilateral rule does not imply, as Homans and Schneider think, the recognition of such future advantages. The most which may be conceded to Homans and Schneider on this score is that Lévi-Strauss does in places speak of "risks," "ambitions," "adventure," and so on with respect to societies which practice one or another rule, as though their members, or even the social systems themselves, made rational appraisals of institutional possibilities. But these expressions, I fear, must be discounted as misplaced psychological rhetoric, or at best as highly figurative characterizations of the systems and of their inherent tendencies to certain kinds of change.[10]

In sum, Lévi-Strauss's theory cannot be described, in the common acceptance of the words, as a "final-cause" theory. Homans and Schneider, indeed, are not using this term in its common acceptance; and they seem to be prepared to admit this when they make the qualification that "for sociology" a theory is a final-cause theory when it claims that an institution is what it is because it is in some sense good for society as a whole—as though notions of causality in sociology were different from those in science in general. Yet the Aristotelian paradigm they quote ("the house is there that men may live in it; but it is also there because the builders have laid one stone upon another") certainly implies

[7] Lévi-Strauss, 1949, pp. 160–64.

[8] Pp. 558–66.

[9] Homans and Schneider, 1955, p. 19.

[10] One place at which Lévi-Strauss does speak of a group exchanging individual advantages for collective security is where he discusses the imbalance wrought in an exchange system, among the Nambikwara, by the chiefly privilege of polygyny (1949, pp. 54–55). But this is clearly figurative, it does not relate to unilateral cross-cousin marriage, and it is an observation which is quite inconsonant with the continuing and explicit theme of his argument.

the factor of purpose; and it is precisely this factor which is lacking in Lévi-Strauss's argument.

If this is the case, though, it has to be asked what ever led Homans and Schneider to think that Lévi-Strauss was arguing in terms of final cause. The answer to this lies in the singular weight which they attach to the following sentence: "The content of the [incest] prohibition is not exhausted by the fact of the prohibition: the latter is instituted only in order to guarantee and found, directly or indirectly, immediately or mediately, an exchange."[11] Their comment on this is: "Note this well: he is not saying that the incest taboo and other marriage rules in fact produce exchanges of women between groups of men, but that the rules exist *because* they produce the exchanges."[12] Now one cannot deny the sense of Lévi-Strauss's assertion in this place, but the question is whether this single sentence exactly reflects the tenor and continuing development of his argument throughout the entire course of his book. The answer is that it does not. There is no other place in the text, I believe, where Lévi-Strauss introduces this purposive element in his analysis of marriage regulations, and certainly not with respect to unilateral cross-cousin marriage. The most with which he may be charged is inconsistency at this point. As far as Homans and Schneider are concerned, however, what we are faced with here is another misrendering similar to that centering on the epithet "better." What they have done is to extract a solitary sentence from a very lengthy and complex exposition, a sentence entirely inconsonant with the clear intent, application, and integral character of Lévi-Strauss's argument, and they have presented it in isolation as though it were characteristic and definitive. Once again, one can only express wonder at such a procedure.

Homans and Schneider further present it as Lévi-Strauss's argument that "if one rule creates more organic solidarity than another, more tribes will adopt it."[13] But from the fact that a rule has superior solidary consequences, it does not follow that it was adopted for that end. Lévi-Strauss himself does not say so, and in the absence of any logical constraint there is no license for in-

[11] Lévi-Strauss, 1949, p. 65.

[12] Homans and Schneider, 1955, p. 4. Authors' italics.

[13] Homans and Schneider, 1955, p. 15.

ferring that this is his intention. There is indeed another possibility, viz., that arrangements with certain solidary advantages stand a greater chance of persisting; and it is not entailed by this circumstance, either, that the superior arrangement was "adopted" with its happy consequences in view. In this connection, Homans and Schneider say of Lévi-Strauss: "He does not use, and in this we think him wise, a survival-value theory: [viz.] we observe today a number of societies following the matrilateral rule because, by reason of having the rule, they were able to survive in competition with other societies."[14] But even this is to put an incorrect and misleading gloss on the possible argument. That such a society survives does not necessarily mean that it successfully competed with other societies: if we are to use the expression, what it could have "competed" with is other forms of social organization, specifically with a patrilateral system; and it is this circumstance that Lévi-Strauss's argument deals with. What Lévi-Strauss is saying, as I interpret his argument, is that some institutions work more effectively than others, and that those which are less effective are less likely to persist. This is a rough phrasing, but I shall take the matter up again later. In this sense, and with the qualification just made, Homans and Schneider are justified in likening Lévi-Strauss's position to a theory of natural evolution; but they are wholly mistaken in ascribing to it, even by implication, a teleological character.[15]

Let us now look at the position as regards efficient causes. It is clear from the discussion of the final causes of the marriage rules in question that Homans and Schneider are mistaken in asserting that for Lévi-Strauss the efficient cause is human intelligence. But he does see the formation of institutions as the unconscious production of "certain fundamental structures of the human mind" by virtue of which human communities tend, in Frazer's words, to "integrate and disintegrate along rigid mathematical lines." He goes out of his way to reject the comparison of human communities with crystals, which was Frazer's simile, but he nevertheless recognizes features of the human mind as constants in social evolution. These features, very briefly, are (1) the demands of the rule as rule; (2) the notion of reciprocity, considered as the most immediate form in which the opposition be-

[14] P. 18.   [15] P. 17.

tween self and others can be integrated; and (3) the character of the gift, such that its transfer from one individual to another changes them into partners and adds a new quality to the valuable which is transferred. Stated in this fashion, the points are inevitably rather obscure, but the central feature is the apprehension by the human mind of reciprocal relations.[16] It is unnecessary for me to expatiate on these matters here, but in these respects it might be claimed that Lévi-Strauss does advance, contrary to what Homans and Schneider say, an efficient-cause theory. These phenomena, he writes, are "fundamental and immediate data of social reality," and must be recognized as "starting points for any attempt at explanation." As I understand him, he maintains that they operate in an unconscious fashion, and that their social products are shaped by the inherent viability or otherwise of their possible permutations. To quote Homans and Schneider's own chosen authority, the situation is as described in Radcliffe-Brown's illuminating statement: "Kinship systems are made and remade by man, in the same sense that languages are made and remade, which does not mean that they are normally constructed or changed by a process of deliberation and under control of a conscious purpose. A language has to work, . . . and in order to work it has to conform to certain general necessary conditions. . . . A kinship system also has to work if it is to exist or persist."[17] This is a parallel which is especially apt to Lévi-Strauss's general position,[18] and I believe it makes his point in this particular context.

It might be objected that the features to which Lévi-Strauss alludes are simply universal grounds for the existence of social institutions, and that in their generality they are incapable of interpretation as differential efficient causes of disparate marriage rules. There is some force in this, but I should tend to think that this argument chiefly exposes the lack of advantage in analyzing Lévi-Strauss's theory in terms of final and efficient causes. In fact, his theory is not a causal theory at all, in either sense. However, as far as the point at issue is concerned, Lévi-Strauss does posit proximate preconditions for the rules in question—though

[16] Lévi-Strauss, 1949, pp. 96, 107, 108, 170–71, 175.

[17] Radcliffe-Brown, 1952, p. 62.

[18] Lévi-Strauss, 1958, chaps. 2–5.

these are not conscious decisions of the human intelligence—and, whether or not they could be termed "efficient causes," these are invoked by him in explanation of the systems based on the rules.

These matters could be argued at length, but it would not be very useful to do so. My intention at this point is simply to claim that, in terms of their central interest in types of causal theory, Homans and Schneider have misunderstood and misrepresented the work they attack. Lévi-Strauss's is not a teleological or deterministic theory, and he does not argue for a final-cause type of sociological explanation; while what might be thought to correspond to efficient cause in his theory is not conscious human intelligence, as Homans and Schneider maintain, but is constituted by unconscious processes of the human mind. Whether or not these positions are valid is not relevant to the matter at issue, which is Homans and Schneider's understanding of the theory which they purport to replace.

II

Homans and Schneider themselves are specifically and solely concerned to propound an efficient-cause theory, and they ask what are the "immediate determinants" of the marriage rules in question. In seeking these, they commit themselves to the formulation of a theory which will "(1) show the relation between different forms of unilateral cross-cousin marriage and other institutions, and (2) cite adequate individual motivation . . . to account for the adoption of a particular marriage rule."[19]

Their theory is of startling simplicity. They begin from the observation that almost all the societies in east Asia which Lévi-Strauss examines are patrilineal, and they ask whether there may not be an association between the type of linearity and the type of unilateral cross-cousin marriage adopted by a society. This suspected connection derives from their notion of the sentimental configurations of the "patrilineal complex," which they take primarily from Radcliffe-Brown's paper, "The Mother's Brother in South Africa" (1924); and their efficient-cause theory, as they explicitly proclaim, derives from this paper.

In the patrilineal complex, to put the matter very summarily, the father has jural authority over the son, and this relationship

[19] Homans and Schneider, 1955, p. 20.

is marked by "respect and constraint" on the part of the latter, while on the other hand the mother does not exercise such jural authority, and she is a "warm and nurturant figure" with whom there is a relationship marked by indulgence. Here we have to refer to Radcliffe-Brown's own propositions. He maintains, it will be remembered, that there is "a tendency to extend to all members of a group a certain type of behaviour which has its origin in a relationship to one particular member of the group." Thus in a patrilineal society a man expects care and indulgence from his mother, and he looks for the same kind of treatment from the people of his mother's group. The way in which this is supposed to happen is as follows: "The pattern of behaviour towards the mother, which is developed in the family by reason of the nature of the family group and its social life, is extended with suitable modifications to the mother's sister and to the mother's brother, then to the group of maternal kindred as a whole, and finally to the maternal gods. . . ." A parallel process is supposed to operate on the other side, to which a man owes obedience and respect. "The patterns that thus arise in relation to the father and the mother are generalized and extended to the kindred on one side and on the other."

As taken over by Homans and Schneider, this theory can be expressed by saying that in the patrilineal complex the mother's brother becomes a kind of male mother, while the father's sister becomes a kind of female father. This leads them to suspect that mother's brother's daughter marriage may be particularly common in patrilineal societies because of the close tie between a man and his mother's brother: "We find in the structure of interpersonal relations the individual motivations, or efficient causes, for the adoption of a particular form of unilateral cross-cousin marriage." Just how this is supposed to come about is of central importance, and much of my argument will relate to the following words:

> As he visits mother's brother often, ego will see a great deal of the daughter: contact will be established. As he is fond of mother's brother, and as mother's brother and his daughter in the patrilineal complex, the Oedipus Complex if you will, are themselves particularly close to one another, he will tend to get fond of the daughter. Their marriage will be sentimentally appropriate. . . .[20]

[20] P. 23.

The same kinds of motives are supposed to make this marriage particularly agreeable to the mother's brother too:

> He takes care of his beloved daughter by giving her to the man in the younger generation to whom he is sentimentally closest, even closer than he is to his own son.[21]

Similarly, the girl tends to be closer to her father than is the son; she identifies her father and his sister; and she tends to find her elder confidante, outside the family of orientation, in her father's sister, who is Ego's mother. "Mother's brother's daughter marriage . . . is sentimentally appropriate for her too."[22]

This argument, as Homans and Schneider themselves state, is in "terms of the motives and behavior of individuals," i.e., it is a psychological argument, instead of in terms of the "norms" which they take to be the objects of Lévi-Strauss's argument; and they attempt to justify this divergence by maintaining that in the long run "behavior determines norms."[23]

So much for matrilateral cross-cousin marriage. A similar situation is supposed to obtain in the case of matrilineal societies, so that "the same kinds of motivation that make matrilateral cross-cousin marriage peculiarly appropriate in patrilineal society make patrilateral cross-cousin marriage peculiarly appropriate in matrilineal society."[24] The locus of jural authority is with the mother's brother rather than with the father; the father is thus an indulgent figure, and so therefore is the father's sister; and hence there is a tendency to marry the father's sister's daughter.

Homans and Schneider's argument is summed up in two propositions, one a special hypothesis and the other a more general theory from which the former is a deduction. They are as follows:

> *Hypothesis.* Societies in which marriage is allowed or preferred with mother's brother's daughter but forbidden or disapproved with father's sister's daughter will be societies possessing patrilineal kin-groups, and societies in which marriage is allowed or preferred with father's sister's daughter but forbidden or disapproved with mother's brother's daughter will be societies possessing matrilineal kin-groups.[25]

> *General theory.* . . . The form of unilateral cross-cousin marriage will be determined by the system of interpersonal

[21] P. 24.
[22] P. 24.
[23] Pp. 25–26.
[24] P. 27.
[25] P. 28.

31

relations precipitated by a social structure, especially by the locus of jural authority over ego. [26]

The authors point out that the connection between the special hypothesis and the general theory is not a necessary one: the hypothesis could be wrong but the theory remain right, or the hypothesis could be right for reasons other than those predicated in the general theory.

With this observation we reach the end of Homans and Schneider's argument up to the point where they proceed to test their own propositions against the ethnographic facts. Accordingly I shall now advance some general criticisms of the argument, and take up the question of empirical test in the next chapter.

III

Homans and Schneider's argument starts from their view of the differential disposition and extension of sentiments in "the patrilineal complex" and in "the matrilineal complex." The former is the commoner, and the more straightforward, so let us begin with it (Fig. 3).

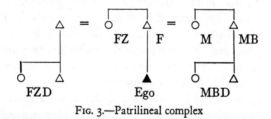

Fig. 3.—Patrilineal complex

Since Homans and Schneider's theory derives, as they tell us, from Radcliffe-Brown's paper on the mother's brother, it must to some extent at least stand or fall with it. How valid, then, is Radcliffe-Brown's argument? This is a matter which has been taken up by a number of scholars, and I do not wish to embark on a tedious detailed recapitulation of their arguments. I shall merely try to show, by reference to these, that Radcliffe-Brown's delineation of the situation is invalid, or at very least undemonstrated. I shall attempt this in the briefest compass, because, tell-

[26] Pp. 28–29.

ing though it is, it is an introductory criticism of Homans and Schneider's position and by no means the most important.

The first pertinent criticism was made by Evans-Pritchard, in an article in which he maintained that the relationships involved are ambiguous, and urged that the influence of the father should be taken into account in considering the formation of the sentiment toward the mother's brother. The latter is not only the mother's brother of Ego, but also the wife's brother of Ego's father. Now the wife's brother is commonly a "pivotal relative" in primitive societies: the attitudes of the husband and the wife are more pronounced toward him than to other relatives, and are more pronouncedly different. It is to be expected, then, that some evidence of this "clash of sentiments" on the part of the parents will be found also in the attitude of Ego to his mother's brother.[27]

Lévi-Strauss himself, in an article first published in 1945 and reissued in slightly amended form in 1958, considerably develops this perceptive argument. The avuncular relationship, he says, is not one of only two terms (MB-ZS),[28] but supposes four, viz., brother, sister, brother-in-law, and nephew; and he maintains that an interpretation such as Radcliffe-Brown's arbitrarily isolates certain elements of a total structure which must be treated as such. The relations in question are, he says, governed by the proposition: "The relation between maternal uncle and nephew is to the relation between brother and sister as the relation between father and son is to that between husband and wife" (MB/ZS:B/Z::F/S:H/W). This generalization holds so well, he claims, that if one pair of relations is known, one can deduce the other. This means, I take it, that one can tell whether the terms in each couple will be of same or opposite sign; that if they are of same sign in one couple they will be of same (though the opposite) sign in the other; and that if the terms are of opposite sign in one couple they will be of opposite sign in the other.

The results of his examination of various societies with unilineal descent may be presented as in Table 1. The plus sign denotes free and familiar relations, and the minus sign relations marked by hostility, antagonism, or reserve. Lévi-Strauss ac-

[27] Evans-Pritchard, 1929.

[28] In the abbreviations of genealogical specifications throughout this book "Z" stands for "sister."

knowledges that these schematic representations of typical relations in each society are not entirely legitimate simplifications, especially since in many systems the relation between two persons is often expressed not by a single attitude but by a number; but he reasonably claims that they can be employed in a provisional fashion, and are acceptable as one stage in the demonstration of his position.

The table, as can be seen, bears out his formula. In opposition to Radcliffe-Brown, who asserts that the rule of descent determines attitudes of opposite character, Lévi-Strauss argues that: "The correlation between forms of avunculate and types of de-

TABLE 1

CONFIGURATIONS OF ATTITUDES

	MB/ZS	B/Z	F/S	H/W
Tcherkesse (patrilineal)	+	+	−	−
Tonga (patrilineal)	+	−	−	+
Kutubu (patrilineal)	−	+	+	−
Dobu (matrilineal)	−	+	+	−
Trobriand (matrilineal)	−	−	+	+
Siuai (matrilineal)	−	+	+	−

scent does not exhaust the problem. Different forms of avunculate can co-exist with one and the same type of descent, patrilineal or matrilineal."[29] If this is so, then however true Homans and Schneider's characterization of the patrilineal complex may be in general, there is no necessary connection between rule of descent and the conventional ascription of sentiments between the four terms in question at the moment. That is, Homans and Schneider's formulation may well hold as an empirical generalization, but it is not—as Lévi-Strauss's is—a structural proposition.

De Heusch criticizes Lévi-Strauss's proposition on the basis of attitudes reported from the Lambumbu of Malekula and the Mundugumor of New Guinea. The scheme of the former is − − + −, and of the latter is + − − −.[30] Clearly, they are in contradiction to the formula. But this does not seem significant, because the Lambumbu are reported to have a bilineal de-

[29] Lévi-Strauss, 1958, pp. 50, 51–52, 55.

[30] De Heusch, 1958, pp. 232–42.

34

scent system, and the Mundugumor are reported to have a system of a quite singular kind which is not clearly described and is most difficult to interpret. If therefore we restrict the scope of Lévi-Strauss's proposition to unilineal descent systems, for which it was designed, it appears to retain its force, and Homans and Schneider's view still gains no support.

De Heusch also makes a more general criticism, emphasizing the difficulty of defining clearly (e.g., by the use of plus and minus signs) relations which are essentially ambivalent. It seems to him that Lévi-Strauss does not take sufficient account of the complexity of the "underlying psychological reality." This charge appears wide of the mark, for we are not concerned with the variable minutiae of the psychic life of individuals (in which all relationships are ambivalent), but with attitudes associated conventionally with jural persons, and these are usually ideally defined in one sense or another by particular cultures. Moreover, if De Heusch's objection were valid it would apply also to the characterization of the relationships in Homans and Schneider's patrilineal complex, so they would gain no support here either.

To return to Radcliffe-Brown's paper, Goody has recently criticized it on three counts. First, that the hypothesis contains no explicit statement of why the generalization of sentiments should not occur in matrilineal societies, in which mothers are presumably no less indulgent of their children than in patrilineal societies. Without dealing with the matrilineal complex itself at this point, clearly this argument tends to undermine Radcliffe-Brown's view of the patrilineal. Second, he observes that no simple hypothesis of the extension of attitudes can account for the considerable variations in behavior between mother's brother and sister's son. Goody's third and major criticism attacks the hypotheses that sentiments are generated in the domestic family and are thence extended outwards, and that a child's behavior towards his mother's brother is an extension of sentiments spontaneously aroused in the child as a direct response to the mother's indulgence, thus concentrating attention on the filial generation. The extension hypothesis, he says, may have some genetic validity in that it gives a hypothetical mechanism whereby the norms of a society are transmitted to a new entrant; but it does not explain why certain extensions ("identifications," as he prefers to phrase it) are made in one society and not in another. Further, to view the process from the point of view of the child gives a one-sided view: it leads to an emphasis on the privileges of the child, while ignoring the counter-rights of the mother's brother. In any case, he remarks, Radcliffe-Brown's theory implies an additional, unstated assumption, that in a patrilineal society a man extends his indulgence from his sister to her child.[31]

Goody makes some other effective points which I shall adduce at appropriate places below. But his criticisms of Lévi-Strauss's contribution, on the contrary, seem to me entirely without basis, and especially since he misrenders Lévi-Strauss's argument. However, to go into these matters here would be an inappropriate digression, taking us away from the main line of the argument.

Finally, Radcliffe-Brown's paper has been the object of a quite different attack on the part of Murdock, who criticizes him for refraining from citing any of the specific ethnographic data and for arguing merely from assumptions. The Bathonga usages in question, he argues, are connected with changes from matrilineal to patrilineal institutions (which was the view against which Radcliffe-Brown specifically directed his paper), and he proposes this historical reconstruction in explanation of them.[32] I do not feel obliged to examine the evidence for this historical argument, or to analyze the structural sequences involved. As recounted by Murdock, the evidence from the ethnography lends his argument plausibility; and if it is indeed the case that the particular usages in question may be related to earlier matrilineal institutions, then the ethnographic example chosen by Radcliffe-Brown loses conviction. I do not imply, though, and could not agree, that the mother's brother-sister's son relationship elsewhere is to be elucidated by historical reconstruction of this sort. My point is that a theory, as propounded, must be judged primarily by the evidence to which it specifically relates; and that if the evidence to which Radcliffe-Brown refers can in fact bear Murdock's interpretation, then his theory is, in respect to that evidence at least, unsatisfactory.

I should remark here, incidentally, that I do not even have to prove that any of the arguments rehearsed here is right. It is enough to list them, in all their forceful plausibility and variety of approaches, and to observe that Homans and Schneider neither

[31] Goody, 1959, pp. 61–62.

[32] Murdock, 1959, pp. 377–78.

mention these considerations nor frame their argument to take account of them.

After this barrage of criticism on the part of others, it is hardly essential for me to make further criticisms of my own of Radcliffe-Brown's paper, but there are certain observations which I think may still be usefully made. The most particular concerns the total lack of evidence for the crucial process of "extension." What empirical reason does Radcliffe-Brown give us to accept his theory? His argument is that the kinship terminology shows it: the term *malume* is supposedly applied "primarily" to the mother's brother and it is also applied—or, as Radcliffe-Brown puts it, is "extended"—to the mother's brother's son. By implication only, it appears that the evidence for this extension is thought to be the fact that if the mother's brother is dead, sacrifices on Ego's behalf are carried out in his place by the mother's brother's son. But this single ritual usage cannot be taken to exhaust the roles of the *malume,* and is therefore exiguous evidence—if it is to be accepted as evidence at all—for the alleged "primary" application of the term. In any case, this supposed process is a simple instance of the extension of a single term to another person of the same sex and line; and it is no evidence at all for the extension of attitudes or "patterns of behavior" from, e.g., a woman in one line (the mother) to a man in another line (the mother's brother). In the Bathonga case Radcliffe-Brown has the temptation of a single radical term applied to both, the mother's brother being a "male mother" (as the term is translated for us), but this is not a general feature of terminologies in patrilineal societies, and is thus no indication of an essential characteristic of "the patrilineal complex."

In fact, of course, and as will be generally agreed today, this instance is no evidence at all for extension of any kind; and the belief that it is derives, as Hocart has best shown,[33] from a prejudice on the part of the European observer. Radcliffe-Brown himself states the real case when he says, in the same place, that nomenclature appropriately reflects "similarity of function"; but he nevertheless insists on trying to explain the genesis of the particular applications of the terms, in spite of the complete lack of any evidence for his assumptions. Indeed, the central objection

[33] Hocart, 1937.

on this score is that, whatever the plausibility or analytical usefulness of the theory, it cannot possibly be tested empirically. It is possible, as Goody notes, to observe the progressive comprehension of a kinship system by a child as it grows up and learns its categories, when it may well learn to use a certain term first for the mother's brother and only afterwards for the latter's son and others sharing the same term; but there is no conceivable evidence for supposing that this process of individual learning re-enacts the formation of the system into which the child is born.

This introduces the consideration that in such a situation, though we may be interested specifically in the mother's brother-sister's son relationship, we are dealing with a *system*. For instance, even if we accept Lévi-Strauss's formulation about the four terms he deals with, there still remains an important figure to be taken into account (as Radcliffe-Brown in fact does), viz., the father's sister. But it is difficult to consider her position usefully without also taking her husband into account, and thence the line to which he belongs and into which she is to some extent incorporated. This done, we are well on the way to covering all the terms comprising the system of categories, and there is no obvious reason to stop at this or at any other intermediate point. In other words, it is arbitrary to isolate two terms (MB, ZS) or four terms, or five or six, from a classification which composes a system and must be analyzed as a system.

Next, the characteristics of a descent system are not exhaustively subsumed under the simple rubric of "patrilineal"; and it is unreasonable to assume, therefore, that the jural or sentimental features of any particular relationship can be deduced, in any particular patrilineal system, from this single elementary feature.

Finally, the topic of rule of descent leads to the consideration of cognatic societies. Radcliffe-Brown deals only with lineal descent systems, and the particular relationship on which he focuses his argument is taken to be characteristic of a patrilineal system; but his starting point, and the source of his entire argument, is the domestic family—and this is not found only in lineal descent systems. If the differentiation and extension of sentiments derive initially, as he asserts, from "the nature of the family group and its social life," then the same processes should be characteristic of cognatic societies as well. Is this true? Well, in the domestic family in cognatic societies it appears to be generally the case that the father is the authoritarian figure and the mother the indulgent figure, just as in the patrilineal situation. But it appears not to be the case, and is not so in certain cognatic societies which I know personally, that the "patterns that . . . arise in relation to the father and the mother are generalized and extended to the kindred on the one side and on the other." It might be objected that in a cognatic society there are no corporate groups defined solely by the rule of descent and which could be unambiguously distinguished as being on one side or the other, and that therefore the theory is not to be expected to apply. But this is not entirely valid. In a cognatic society it is as a matter of fact often possible, and may even be usual, to distinguish paternal and maternal relatives, with little or no overlap; and any great overlap is to be expected only in special circumstances (small groups, local endogamy), not in cognatic societies in general, and certainly not in any structurally necessary fashion.

Radcliffe-Brown's argument should then apply to relationships in a cognatic society as much as to those in a patrilineal society, but it does not. It is true that the mother's brother is not generally an authoritarian figure like the father, and obviously so since he has not the position of jural authority in Ego's domestic family. But this distinction does not in itself mean very much. A more revealing opposition is that between the father's brother (who in a patrilineal society will commonly be a "father," with at least latent authority over Ego) and the mother's brother; and here we find that in certain cognatic societies at least (Penan, rural Malays, Sarakatsani) no terminological distinction is made between them, and that no distinct conventional attitudes are appropriate to them. The same considerations apply to the mother's sister and the father's sister, and even more revealingly since they are specific examples in Radcliffe-Brown's argument. Nor is there any terminological or jural distinction between mother's brother's child and father's sister's child. Yet if the relations with these relatives on the father's side and on the mother's were indeed, as Radcliffe-Brown claims, "the product of the social life within the family in the narrow sense" these two classes of relatives should be jurally and sentimentally distinguished as clearly as in a patrilineal system. So far as I can discover, and within my own experience, they are not. Note, too, that I have been speaking of close genealogically defined individuals, not of whole categories of kin, and even so the theory does not hold. On this count as well, then, Radcliffe-Brown's extension theory to account for jural and sentimental distinctions in a patrilineal society cannot be accepted.

All these arguments combine to show at very least that there is no simple, universal, or necessary patrilineal complex such as Radcliffe-Brown delineates, and which Homans and Schneider adopt as the very foundation of their argument; and that Radcliffe-Brown's theory of extension to explain the differential attribution of sentiment and jural status in a patrilineal society is fallacious. To the extent, then, that Homans and Schneider's theory rests on these notions, it must be mistaken.

IV

There are still further formal arguments against their theory, though, before we even get down to examining the ethnographic facts which will finally settle the matter.

The father's sister is an important figure in the patrilineal situation, both in fact and in Homans and Schneider's argument. Have they correctly considered her position and her possible influence in the negotiation of marriages? The point at issue is the alleged association of tense respect with jural authority. Homans and Schneider argue from the premise that "the locus of jural authority over ego . . . will at least lie within ego's own lineage."[34] Granted this, how is the position of the father's sister to be defined? They argue, it will be recalled, that she is a kind of female father and so is treated with distance and respect; that this attitude will be extended to her daughter; and that therefore marriage with the father's sister's daughter will not be "sentimentally appropriate." Whether or not the father's sister's daughter is married, then, depends on the jural and/or sentimental identification of the father's sister with the father. Let us look at this proposition.

In a patrilineal system (see Fig. 3 again) authority over Ego will normally lie, as Homans and Schneider posit, within Ego's own lineage and specifically with his father. Then, either (1) the father's sister is regarded as a member of this lineage, shares this

---

[34] Homans and Schneider, 1955, p. 29.

authority, and therefore is treated with respect, or (2) she is regarded as a member of her husband's lineage, in which case there is by definition no relationship of authority to be marked by respect.

If (1) is the case, the situation is irrelevant to the possibility of marriage with the father's sister's daughter, for then there will be no occasion for the lineal identification of the father's sister with her daughter, since they belong to different lineages. Whether marriage with the father's sister's daughter would be sentimentally appropriate might therefore rest on whether the sentiment towards the father's sister is "extended" to her husband, the person who possesses jural authority over the girl, but this is not part of Homans and Schneider's theory as stated. If (2) is the case, on the other hand, the father's sister does not share in the jural authority of the father over Ego, there is thus no occasion for any attitude of reserve which might be extended to her and thence to her daughter, and marriage with the father's sister's daughter might very well therefore be sentimentally appropriate. That is, if we are to agree that the mother's brother's daughter may be married because the mother's brother, like the mother, does not have jural authority over Ego, we have also to conclude that the father's sister's daughter may equally well be married for the same kind of reason.

It may be objected, however, that the issue is not whether the father's sister personally possesses authority over Ego, but that she is in some sense identified with someone (viz., her brother) who does. But this brings us back to the extension theory, and as we have seen we have been given no reason to accept it.

So far, then, we see that an argument based on a necessary association of authority and adverse sentiment breaks down. May it not be the case, though, that the sentiment of reserve and respect associated with the father nonetheless happens to be associated with the father's sister also, even though she has not the authority which is the presumed cause of the tense and distant relationship? This may certainly be so, but it is doubtful that this circumstance would help Homans and Schneider's argument. Assuming this feeling, is there any reason to suppose that it will further be "extended" to the father's sister's daughter? One would immediately think not, as we observed above. The father's sister, whatever the degree of her incorporation into her husband's lineage, and her daughter do not in any respect occupy equivalent statuses (as, for example, may the mother's brother and his son). The marriage of the daughter will remove her from her mother (Ego's father's sister); she cannot succeed to the father's sister's status within the group into which the latter has been married; and especially after her own marriage she can claim no position in the group from which her mother came. What then would be the basis for a lineal identification—comparable to that of mother's brother with mother's brother's son—which would bring about the application of the same attitude to both women? I think that in general there is likely to be none, and that therefore there is no need to accede to Homans and Schneider's assumption that marriage with the father's sister's daughter would in this circumstance be sentimentally inappropriate.

Similarly, even if it were true, and demonstrable, that the conventional attitude toward the mother's brother derives from that toward the mother, so that Ego likes the mother's brother, is it really entailed that he will also tend to like the mother's brother's daughter? I do not deny, of course, that in particular cases he may do so, but is this a necessary or general extension of the sentiment in question? Homans and Schneider do no more than assert that "as he is fond of mother's brother . . . he will tend to get fond of the daughter."[35] But this is a crucial step in the extension process posited, and it is essential that it be argued, not just flatly asserted as though there could be no doubt in the matter.

Further, if the mother's brother's daughter is married because of the close and warm relationship with the mother's brother, what about the tense and distant relationship with the wife's father such as is so commonly found? Homans and Schneider admit the general character of the latter relationship: "the relationship between father-in-law and son-in-law is only less 'difficult' than the mother-in-law relationships," but they have what they consider an answer. "We argue . . . that ego's tie with mother's brother *before* the latter becomes father-in-law is primary in influence as it is in time, and that one good reason why ego might want to marry his daughter is that the established relationship will soften the asperities of an otherwise 'difficult' situation."[36] I

[35] P. 23. [36] P. 25.

42

should prefer to say that they do not argue, but merely assert, that this is the case; for there is another immediate possibility, and it is the resolution of this logical situation in one sense or the other which really has to be argued. It might be urged, namely, that Ego values his close association with the mother's brother and that hence he will decline to convert the relationship into one of tense distance by marrying the latter's daughter. This is just as plausible a formulation as Homans and Schneider's. Which of the two is more just is indeed a matter for argument, and for empirical demonstration, but our authors give no indication of realizing this, or of the grounds on which they would reach a decision.

We are now more forcibly obliged to consider whether all this emphasis on sentiments is important at all. Which is the factor the more likely to predominate in the contraction of a union between two lineal descent groups—sentiment, or authority? As sociologists, or lawyers, or as men of common sense, we should confidently conclude upon the latter. Such a union is, we know well, not a mere coming together of two like-minded individuals, in which case (as in Europe and America) sentiment may play a predominant part. It is commonly an *alliance* between two autonomous groups of men, inaugurated by the betrothal and continuing for as long as the duration of the union. The alliance may entail involvement in war or feud, material responsibility in the redress of wrongs, contribution to marriage payments, economic co-operation, and religious interdependence. Is it likely that such grave and consequential affairs in the polity of a simple society should be determined by individual sentiments of the kinds delineated by Homans and Schneider? The probability, I think, is that sentiments will be negligible factors, and especially on the parts of certain individuals to whom Homans and Schneider ascribe them, viz., Ego, the father's sister, and the female cross-cousins.

At this point we return to the importance of the status of the father's sister. It will be generally agreed, with Leach,[37] that marriages are typically the concern of local groups of coresident males. Where does the father's sister fit into this picture? We may accept as premise that the father possesses jural authority over his children, male and female. His wife, a stranger from another

[37] Leach, 1951, p. 24.

43

group, is without such authority, and is moreover characterized as an indulgent figure. Now the father's sister is herself such a woman in the group into which she has been married; and whatever the sentiment conventionally associated with her, and whether or not it is attached to her daughter also, she has not generally the authority to give her daughter in marriage. It is the girl's father, Ego's father's sister's husband, who has to be reckoned with. And who may be expected to deal with him? Not Ego, but Ego's father and perhaps other senior men of the same group. What Ego's conventionally defined sentiments may be, then—either toward his father's sister or toward her husband or toward the father's sister's daughter—are, institutionally speaking, immaterial. The really important relationship in the contraction of marriage is one from which he is excluded, viz., that between his father and the sister's husband of the latter. If sentiments are of any causal effect, therefore, it is in this affinal relationship that their place must be determined; but, as we have seen, such a consideration has neither practical importance nor analytical advantage in any of the respects proposed by Homans and Schneider.

We must conclude, then, that even in the case of the supposed sentimentally inappropriate marriage (that with the father's sister's daughter) individual motivations of the sorts suggested cannot be decisive. But our authors could erect one last line of defense. Even if the situation, jurally and sentimentally, is as I have analyzed it, so that marriage to mother's brother's daughter and marriage to father's sister's daughter are in many respects equivalent, the former may still possess an advantage derived from the sentiments they isolate. That is, the agreed non-authoritarian relationship with the mother's brother is different from that with the father's sister's husband in a way which may tip the balance in favor of the matrilateral practice. The maternal uncle is, after all, the brother of Ego's mother: the father's sister's husband is a stranger, i.e., not necessarily a cognatic relative at all. But this argument would have force only if we admitted Homans and Schneider's decision to restrict the application of their theory to first cousins. In fact, however, a term which is conventionally translated as "mother's brother's daughter" may in any particular patrilineal society denote a large class of individuals. Would Homans and Schneider then claim that the sentiments they distinguish characterize significantly all "mother's brothers" and all their daughters, to such a degree as to divert marital proceedings away from all the "father's sister's husbands" and their daughters? We do not know, because of the unrealistic limitation they have placed on the connotations of the kinship terms in question; but if they did make this claim they would have to propose an extension theory of an application dwarfing all previous considerations. However, they have not done so, and we are thereby relieved of the necessity to mount a further attack on the theory of extensions. The point is very important, though, and we shall return to it in chapter 4. For the moment, I may allow myself one comment which would have had less force if made earlier: it is precisely this restriction of the scope of their argument to first cousins which initially and most significantly betrays to us Homans and Schneider's disregard of the systems of categories which their theory is intended to elucidate. This doctrinaire neglect of the facts of the case—here, the connotations of the categories for the people who employ them and who order their lives by them—is the gravest defect in their enterprise.

V

It would be wearisome and is unnecessary to investigate these points all over again in criticizing Homans and Schneider's view of the matrilineal complex, and some brief comments will suffice. In a matrilineal system (Fig. 4) the situation is in many respects the reverse of that in a patrilineal system. ". . . The same kinds of motivation that make matrilateral cross-cousin marriage appropriate in patrilineal society make patrilateral cross-cousin marriage peculiarly appropriate in matrilineal society."[38] Our authors acknowledge that this motivation will not lead to effective results as often in matrilineal as in patrilineal societies, for the reason that in the latter Ego depends for his wife on a man (the mother's brother), while in the former he depends on his ties with the father's sister, "and a woman may well have less power of disposing of her daughter than a man." This is said to be because women are in general jurally subordinate to men, so that a matrilineal society can never be the mirror image of a patrilineal society. They believe, nevertheless, that the forces at work will

---

[38] Homans and Schneider, 1955, p. 27.

be strong enough in some matrilineal societies to create a "prefer-ence" for marriage to the father's sister's daughter.

They do not say what these forces are, or how they apply, but they seem to have in mind something like the following situation. Ego is under the jural control of his mother's brother, and his relationship with him is therefore one of distance and respect. Consequently this attitude is extended to the mother's brother's daughter, and marriage with her will therefore be sentimentally inappropriate. On the other hand, his father and father's sister are indulgent figures, and his relationship with them is close and affectionate. Consequently this attitude is extended to the father's sister's daughter, and she is therefore the woman with whom marriage is sentimentally appropriate.

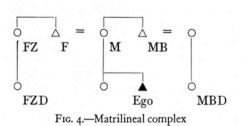

Fig. 4.—Matrilineal complex

But two awkward points now arise. Homans and Schneider maintain that in a matrilineal society it is through ties with a woman, the father's sister, that the wife is to be obtained; and they even concede a weakness in their theory on this score. But this is not the case at all. In this matrilineal complex, as we know to be commonly the case, it is still men who possess jural au-thority—in this case, over their sisters' children, male and female. It is therefore Ego's father who has authority over the father's sister's daughter; and if the relationship with him is close and affectionate we have a precise sentimental parallel to the position of the mother's brother in a patrilineal society. That is, marriage with the father's sister's daughter in a matrilineal society may be held to be sentimentally appropriate because the relationship with the man who has authority over her is non-authoritarian and affectionate. Homans and Schneider's theory thus fares better than they think, but hardly in a manner conducive to confidence, since their own formulation rests on an inadequate analysis of the relationships involved.

46

The second point is more serious. We have no evidential grounds for supposing that in a matrilineal society a mother is any less indulgent than in a patrilineal society. Authority is indeed vested in her side of the family, but in her brother, not in herself. What happens to the extension theory then? According to Radcliffe-Brown the attitude to the mother should be generalized and extended to the mother's brother, but here it is not: the relationships are of opposite character. The case is not so clear on the other side, but while the ethnography suggests that the father in a matrilineal society is commonly an indulgent figure, the father's sister in a number of such societies (e.g., Ashanti, Kaguru, Mota, Siuai) is treated with marked respect. Homans and Schneider's theory, as they themselves present it, then sustains another blow; for in this case also marriage with the father's sister's daughter must on their premises be sentimentally inappropriate, in a matrilineal as well as in a patrilineal society. This is a damaging objection, but what is far more important is that this system of relationships as a whole constitutes a further invalidation of the theory of sentiments which is central to Homans and Schneider's argument.

There exist admittedly other matrilineal societies (e.g., Hopi, Trobriands) in which the father's sister is in fact a close and indulgent figure, and which do therefore fit Homans and Schneider's scheme. But these cases do not so much support their argument as confirm in another respect Lévi-Strauss's analysis of the variant configurations of conventional attitudes in unilineal descent systems. That is, there is no simple, universal or necessary matrilineal complex, any more than there is a patrilineal; so that it is not possible to infer from the mere rule of descent what sentimental or jural position will be occupied by the father's sister in a matrilineal society, or whether marriage with her daughter will or will not be sentimentally appropriate.

At this point, to be fair, we have to abandon our orderly progress through Homans and Schneider's argument and skip ahead to near the end of it, where they encounter the same issue. They have been discussing certain matrilineal societies which, contrary to their hypothesis, marry the matrilateral cross-cousin. The hypothesis, they say, derived from their assumption that in matrilineal societies jural authority would always be vested in the mother's brother, "and this is not the case." That is, they engagingly proceed, "we assumed, when we ought to have known better, that there was only one main matrilineal complex—the Trobriand type—whereas in fact there are at least two."[39] By this conclusion they appear to have forestalled, however belatedly, the objection just raised, but the position is not quite so simple. In distinguishing two complexes, Homans and Schneider refer to the factors of domicile and marital residence. In one complex, a man lives with his mother's brother before marriage and brings his wife there; in the other, he lives with his father before marriage and then goes to his wife's place. These, of course, are important differences, particularly with respect to the exercise and influence of jural authority before marriage; for in the latter case, "Interpersonal relations much resemble those of the patrilineal complex." However, Homans and Schneider deal at this point only with the relationships with the father and the mother's brother—but they have not mentioned the crucial figure of the father's sister, the sentimental ties with whom are supposed to induce a man to marry her daughter. Yet it is precisely her position which cannot be taken for granted. My point, again, is that we cannot simply infer from the jural character of the mother's brother, or from the attitude to the father, what the relationship with the father's sister will be, either in the former matrilineal complex or in the latter.

This whole issue may be further exposed by pursuing the indications given above about the Siuai. This means, for once, using an ethnographic source which Homans and Schneider could not have consulted, since it was published in the same year as their own book; but usable indications to the same effect could be cited from other sources, so there is no reason to refrain from using the best. This is Oliver's monograph on the Siuai, which contains admirably explicit data on the points at issue.

Descent among the Siuai is matrilineal. A man usually lives in his father's hamlet until the latter's death, when he tends to move to his "matrilineal center," where his maternal uncle may be. Marital residence, with reference to the hamlet, is predominantly virilocal.[40] As far as domicile and marital residence are concerned, therefore, the Siuai do not fit either of Homans and Schneider's matrilineal complexes. Nor do they fit with regard

[39] P. 47. [40] Oliver, 1955, pp. 237, 163.

to the configuration of attitudes. The father is a relatively indulgent figure, and there is a closer affective tie with him than with the mother's brother. The latter is held in "awe," and a man is more likely to obey him than his own father. "Maternal uncles assert their authority frequently and forcefully." So far, so good: a "typical" matrilineal situation, we might say. But when we turn to the father's sister we find that the "most noteworthy feature of this relationship is *avoidance*."[41] So here we have a matrilineal system with authority and respect on one side (mother's brother) and avoidance on the other (father's sister)—yet "marriage with mother's brother's daughter is preferred to all other forms."[42]

In sum, this is a system which is recalcitrant in nearly all respects to Homans and Schneider's premises and argument. First, it constitutes quite another kind of matrilineal complex than the two at which they eventually arrive. Second, it controverts the extension theory, in that while the mother is apparently indulgent the mother's brother is an authoritarian figure, and that while the father is a close and permissive relative the father's sister is avoided: i.e., the relatives on each side, far from being sentimentally identified, are of opposite characters. Third, the preferred marriage is contrary to Homans and Schneider's general theory in that it is with the side where jural authority lies.

All this goes to show that matrilineal societies exhibit very considerable variation one from another, in regard to domicile, marital residence, jural authority, and configuration of attitudes. Far from being able to argue on the basis of "the matrilineal complex" initially postulated by Homans and Schneider and resorted to throughout the greater part of their argument, we must in fact be prepared to recognize a fair number of distinct types, to only one of which may their central argument usefully apply. I would offer the suggestion, incidentally, that these variations may in themselves be signs of certain inherent difficulties in constituting a social system based on matriliny, a matter to which we shall return later.

Finally, an expository comment on Homans and Schneider's ultimate recognition that there is not only one matrilineal com-

[41] Oliver, 1955, pp. 251, 257; author's italics.

[42] Oliver, 1955, p. 153.

plex. I personally find it highly interesting to be conducted by them through the several steps by which they reach their final position, and for me it is one of their book's chief attractions that it has the character of work-notes. But it must be conceded that it is rather odd that, having carried out the investigations they report, and having then realized that one of their vital premises was mistaken, our authors should have rehearsed in their publication the whole progress of their lucubrations. One may warm to their candid admission that they ought to have known better, but remain ungrateful for having been obliged to follow an erroneous line of argument for so long once they did.

VI

The last formal argument that I wish to advance is the most general. It is that if the sentiments in question are so completely general in lineal descent systems, they cannot explain (account for the "adoption," the existence, of) a marital institution which appears with such rarity among them. "The psychological factor is too general to predetermine the course of social phenomena. Since it does not imply one social form rather than another, it cannot explain any."[43] It should be noted especially that this criticism relates particularly to Homans and Schneider's general theory, which holds that "the form of unilateral cross-cousin marriage will be determined by" certain personal relations, and especially by the locus of authority. The special hypothesis merely postulates two simple *correlations* of linearity of descent groups with laterality of marriage; but the general theory is a *causal* proposition purporting to isolate the efficient causes that "determine" the "adoption" of one or the other form of unilateral cross-cousin marriage. That is, given a lineal descent system with a certain locus of authority, the consequent disposition of sentiments is the efficient cause of the adoption of the rule of marriage. It is true that at one point Homans and Schneider write: "*Given* unilateral cross-cousin marriage, . . . What will determine the adoption of one form of unilateral cross-cousin marriage rather than the other?"[44] But this proviso relates specifically to the spe-

[43] Durkheim, 1901, p. 133.

[44] Homans and Schneider, 1955, p. 28; authors' italics.

cial hypothesis, not to the general theory. In fact, of course, the proviso cannot really apply to the special hypothesis, since the latter simply asserts correlations, not processes; but this is what Homans and Schneider actually write, and what they must be presumed to mean. On the other hand, it could not qualify the general theory either, since it would be meaningless to premise a causal proposition on the existence of that which was said to be caused by its terms. It might be replied that what Homans and Schneider really mean (though it is not what they say) is that given a certain locus of authority, and given an unspecified form of unilateral cross-cousin marriage, they can infer from the disposition of the sentiments the side with which such marriage is actually practiced. But this would be merely to state the sentimental contexts of the rules correlated in the special hypothesis: it would not isolate the efficient causes which determined the adoption of one or the other rule of marriage.

This being the case, we have in Homans and Schneider's general theory a causal proposition which, literally, states the origin of each form of unilateral cross-cousin marriage. Leaving aside the question of what would count as evidence, the first consideration is that if the sentiments, as delineated by Homans and Schneider, were indeed effective in bringing about the adoption of such an institution in lineal descent systems, then it would be far more common in such systems than it is. Here I begin to turn, with some relief, to particular facts. Homans and Schneider report that they tested their hypothesis against the data on the 250 societies used by Murdock in his *Social Structure*.[45] In only fifteen of these societies is unilateral cross-cousin marriage clearly reported, twelve being matrilateral and three patrilateral.[46] Homans and Schneider accordingly observe that, if the sample is representative, either form of unilateral cross-cousin marriage must be a "rare phenomenon," but they do not draw any inference about the consequences of this fact for their general theory. They make a methodological slip, incidentally, in relating this small number of cases to the total of 250 societies in the sample; for only 175 have lineal descent systems, to which alone their hypothesis applies, so that the rarity of the institution is not

[45] Murdock, 1949.

[46] Homans and Schneider, 1955, pp. 30–31.

quite so marked as they think. Nevertheless, it is still rare, as is shown by an examination of the 360 lineal descent systems in Murdock's world ethnographic sample. Of these, only sixteen practice "cross-cousin marriage with patrilateral preference" and only forty-nine with a "matrilateral preference."[47] That is, even framing the question in Homans and Schneider's own terms, viz., by "preferences," only 18 per cent of the societies in this larger sample practice unilateral cross-cousin marriage. Their general theory is thus in violation of one of the first methodological rules of all science, in that it purports to explain facts of low incidence by factors of high generality.[48]

Moreover, there is the distinction between preference and prescription to be taken into account in assessing the general theory of the determination of the rule of marriage. Take, for example, a patrilineal society with its correlated matrilateral rule of marriage. This rule may be preferential, or it may be prescriptive; so that, even if the sentiments determined the side with which marriage was contracted, "there would be no need for matrilateral marriage to be *prescribed*."[49] There is nothing in such general sentiments which could reasonably be held to determine the adoption of so distinctive a rule as a matrilateral prescription. In fact, even if we made the maximum concession to Homans and Schneider's argument, it could at very most indicate that certain sentiments may be the grounds of the marriage regulations. Logically, they are not and cannot be the efficient causes of either preference or prescription, matrilateral rule or patrilateral.

[47] Murdock, 1957, p. 687.

[48] "The worldwide incidence of such preferences . . . is so low as to cast some doubt on the validity of the theoretical interpretation advanced" (Murdock, 1957, p. 687).

[49] Lévi-Strauss, 1958, pp. 344–45. Note especially the author's italics; cf. chap. 1, sec. II.

Chapter Three

> Talk about one thing at a time. That is, in choosing your words (or, more pedantically, concepts) see that they refer not to several classes of fact at the same time but to one and one only.—HOMANS[1]

EVIDENCE

Here we leave general considerations and take up the examination of the facts.

I

Homans and Schneider test their hypothesis against a total of thirty-three societies.[2] They do not claim that this is a complete list of societies practicing "unilateral cross-cousin marriage," but only as many as they could conveniently discover without making an exhaustive search of the literature beyond what they considered the point of diminishing returns.

Since they confuse prescription and preference, our first task is to isolate those societies which *prescribe* unilateral cross-cousin marriage. The clearest procedure is to work through their list, in the order in which they arrange the societies and under their own headings. Like our authors, I shall not justify my decision in each case, though I am prepared to do so if challenged, and intend in any case to publish separate analyses of certain difficult or illuminating cases. Nor shall I cite, for the most part, any ethnographic sources. I have used, in the first instance, those cited by Homans and Schneider,[3] so that my conclusions shall at least relate to the same evidence as they examine. If the ethnography indicates reliably that a system is non-prescriptive, I have usually gone no further into the literature, since this means that it is not of the type to which Lévi-Strauss's and Homans and Schneider's theories apply in common and is therefore to be excluded from further discussion. For the prescriptive instances, my characteriza-

---

[1] Homans, 1951, p. 16.

[2] Homans and Schneider, 1955, p. 34. [3] Pp. 62–63.

tions rest in the majority of cases on an examination of every available published source of information; and in cases where the literature is too vast for this to be feasible (Batak), or is mainly in a language which I cannot read (Gilyak), on as extensive a survey of the more renowned and comprehensive accounts as proved practicable.

I have to observe that Homans and Schneider's work in this respect is defective in that they rely in nearly every case on a single ethnographic source, and even this is sometimes not the most useful. For example, there are many hundreds of references on the Batak, stretching back to the fifteenth century, and it is an exiguous procedure to consult only one. Moreover, there are good modern monographs dealing specifically with matrilateral alliance among the Batak, yet Homans and Schneider rely on a slim and secondary article. They cite one article on the Karadjeri, but there are at least thirteen other references, three of which are essential supplements to the source actually used, and all of these have to be employed if an adequate analysis of the Karadjeri system is to be made. As a final example, Homans and Schneider do indeed cite the most comprehensive and useful single source on the Thado, but there are twenty-eight other useful references, and a number of these are indispensable to an adequate analysis. Their procedure is even less easy to understand in the cases of societies such as the Lovedu and the Miwok, on which very few ethnographical accounts of sociological value exist.

I do not intend by these comments, however, to imply that Homans and Schneider have actually characterized incorrectly, by the two criteria of their classification (rule of descent group constitution, laterality of marriage), the societies that they examine. My point is that, as a matter of principle, it is not possible to reach sure conclusions in this way. To use a single source may give the right answers—but it may very well not. Moreover, while Homans and Schneider are primarily concerned, in their classification, to test a hypothesis correlating the features involved, they proceed to examine the correlations by reference to jural authority, sentiments, bridewealth, domicile, marital residence, corporate groups, associations, etc., in an attempt to validate their general theory. But to do this properly it is essential to make as thorough a survey as possible of all available facts. It is a methodological regression, and especially for reasons which will be apparent in the next chapter, simply to isolate a limited number of institutional variables without making a systematic investigation in each case in order to assess their significance, sentimental or other, in the societies from which they are reported. Of course, if a comparison of a large number of societies is to be undertaken, it means a great deal of work and a protracted investigation to master the entire corpus of evidence on each one; but ultimately it is the only scholarly thing to do.

These, anyway, are the societies of Homans and Schneider's sample:

1. *"Patrilineages—matrilateral form preferred"*:

Altaians and Teleuts: Non-prescriptive.

Batak: Prescriptive.

Gilyak: Prescriptive.[4]

Gold: Prescriptive.

Kachin: Prescriptive.

Karadjeri: Not prescriptive in the sense required. They have a four-section system, and although marriage with the genealogical father's sister's daughter is forbidden they marry categorically a bilateral cross-cousin.

Lakher: Non-prescriptive, to judge by the explicit ethnographic reports concerning marriage. The relationship terminology recorded in one source is that of a matrilateral prescriptive system; but taken as a whole the ethnographic data are inconsistent and do not permit the sure inference that this is a system of prescriptive alliance.

Lhota: Non-prescriptive.

Limba: Non-prescriptive.

Lovedu: Prescriptive.

Mbundu: Non-prescriptive.

Mende: Non-prescriptive.

Miwok: Prescriptive.

Murngin: Not prescriptive in the sense required, but a very difficult case. There is indeed a categorical distinction between MBD and FZD, and the latter may not be married. But they also have an eight-section system (though in certain respects, as Warner shows, it resembles a four-section

---

[4] Sternberg, in Lévi-Strauss, 1949, chap. 18.

system), and marriage is thus necessarily with a genealogically bilateral cross-cousin.

Rengma: Non-prescriptive.

Sandawe: Non-prescriptive.

Sema: Non-prescriptive.

Thado: Prescriptive.

Timne: Non-prescriptive.

Venda: Prescriptive.

Wik-Munkan (Archer River group) : Not prescriptive in the sense required. A straightforward two-section system with exogamous moieties, plus differentiation of senior and junior affines. The genealogical FZD is forbidden, but marriage is categorically with a bilateral cross-cousin.

Yir-Yoront: A difficult case, but not certainly unilaterally prescriptive. MBD and FZD are categorically distinguished, and marriage with the latter is forbidden. Patrilineal moieties; one strictly exogamous, the other endogamous with respect to certain of its clans. The pattern and extension of the terminology is unlike that of any certainly matrilateral prescriptive system, and its identification of alternate generations suggests a bilineal section-system. I will concede that to represent this as a unilateral prescriptive system is, as far as the explicit evidence goes, defensible; but such a conclusion is by no means clear or indubitable and I shall not list it as such.

2. *"Patrilineages—patrilateral form preferred"*:

Kandyu: Non-prescriptive. Exogamous moieties, but no bilineal sections. Marriage appears to be with a bilateral cross-cousin, with the qualifications that the matrilateral first cousin may not be married, nor the daughter of the father's elder sister. Marriage is reported permitted with a classificatory MBD.

Sherente: A difficult case with confusing and doubtful ethnographic details, but not prescriptive in the sense required.

3. *"Matrilineages—matrilateral form preferred"*:

Garo: Non-prescriptive.

Kaonde: Non-prescriptive.

Kaska: Unclear and incomplete ethnography in the relevant respects, but apparently not prescriptive in the sense required.

Sirionó: Prescriptive.

4. *"Matrilineages—patrilateral form preferred"*:
Haida: Non-prescriptive.
Ila: Non-prescriptive.
Tismulun: Unclear ethnography; MBD may not be married, but unilateral cross-cousin marriage is not prescribed.
Tlingit: Non-prescriptive.
Trobrianders: Non-prescriptive.

Perhaps I should stress that the characterizations "prescriptive" and "non-prescriptive" refer only to unilateral cross-cousin marriage. Thus the Karadjeri certainly have a prescriptive marriage system (viz., a four-section system), but marriage is non-prescriptive as far as either unilateral cross-cousin is concerned and preferential with regard to the mother's brother's daughter.

TABLE 2

PRESCRIBED MARRIAGE AND LINEARITY

PRESCRIBED MARRIAGE	DESCENT	
	Patrilineal	Matrilineal
Matrilateral.............	8	1
Patrilateral.............	...	...

The results of this survey are as in Table 2, which should be compared with Homans and Schneider's Table 1.[5] The immediate conclusions are clear and forceful: (1) only nine out of Homans and Schneider's thirty-three societies (or 27 per cent) practice prescriptive unilateral cross-cousin mariage; (2) not one society in their sample practices prescriptive patrilateral cross-cousin marriage.

Now Homans and Schneider claim to explain *both* types of "unilateral cross-cousin marriage." The argument is about prescriptions, and their theory applies in part (specifically, not only by the fact of contending with Lévi-Strauss) to prescriptions. But when we examine their test cases we see that they have no prescriptive patrilateral cases at all. Their own evidence thus relates to only *one* form of prescriptive marriage, and cannot therefore yield any support whatever for their claim to explain the differential incidence of both types.

[5] Homans and Schneider, 1955, p. 34.

But this demonstration does not entirely undermine Homans and Schneider's position. One proposition in their hypothesis, after all, is that the matrilateral rule will be found with patrilineal descent groups; and even if there are no patrilateral cases to test the other part of the hypothesis, we still have in the figures what appears to be a significant preponderance of patrilineal-marilateral instances in favor of this proposition. Sticking to these societies for the moment, therefore, let us examine the evidence further in terms of the argument by which Homans and Schneider explain this correlation.

A preliminary consideration is that something of the uncertainty entailed by Homans and Schneider's inadequate use of the ethnographic literature is reflected in their reports on this class of societies. On the point of jural authority, they report: "For none of the patrilineal-matrilateral societies, except the Murngin and Yir-Yoront, . . . is there reason to suspect that the locus of immediate jural authority over ego lies in any person but his father." On the position of the mother's brother: "For thirteen of these societies . . . the reported data suggest, in our view, a relationship between ego and mother's brother that has at least some points in common with the relationship in the classic patrilineal complex. . . ." And concerning the father's sister, though they do at least feel confident enough to claim that "she appears in the role we expected from our general theory," they cite only four societies in which this is said to be the case, and of these just one is a prescriptive instance. As for all the societies not cited with regard to one or other of these relationships, "we have been unable to consult the Russian sources personally, and the rest do not provide adequate information on interpersonal relationships." Finally, the only particular facts adduced in confirmation of the theory, viz., those reported from the Lovedu, are cited simply by way of "illustration": nothing concerning the other societies of the class can legitimately be inferred from them, and we are thus left with explicit evidence on only one single society. Leaving aside the question of whether a more thorough investigation of the ethnography on each society might not have yielded evidence of the sort Homans and Schneider were looking for, these are remarkably inexplicit, tentative, and partial grounds on which to base an assertion that this class of societies conforms both to their special hypothesis and to their general theory.[6]

Again, I do not intend to controvert their characterization of this class of societies in general with regard to the relationships in question, but to draw attention to the character of what they present as evidence. Consider particularly the report concerning the relationship with the mother's brother. The patrilineal-matrilateral class comprises twenty-two societies, but Homans and Schneider feel able to cite only thirteen of them in support of their general theory. Of these, only four actually prescribe marriage with the matrilateral cross-cousin. And with regard to the mother's brother, they can say nothing more definite than that the data "suggest, in our view, a relationship . . . that has at least some points in common" with what they postulate. In other words, as far as this crucial relationship is concerned, the initially impressive number of allegedly confirmatory test cases is diminished by nearly half, further reduced to only four prescriptive instances; and instead of real evidence we are offered little more than vague, qualified, and inconclusive impressions.

At this point it may be of interest to look at the matter of evidence with respect to the Yir-Yoront, which is one of the two patrilineal-matrilateral societies which Homans and Schneider regard as exceptions to their general theory, in that they understand the locus of authority to be elsewhere than they think it should be. I agree with them that the Murngin do not constitute a true exception; but I think that in treating the Yir-Yoront as a "full exception" they misread the evidence to the detriment of their own case. Their conclusion is based on the facts that the father is an affectionate figure, while the discipline of young children devolves on the mother, and that the mother's brother is regarded with great respect. They therefore infer that it is the mother's brother who is "the chief male authority over ego."

But this is an unjustified conclusion. Neither on the page of the article which they cite nor elsewhere in the ethnographic literature is it reported that this is the case, or even that the mother's brother shares the role of disciplinarian with the mother, as Homans and Schneider assert. Then they overlook the distinction between domestic control over a young child and jural authority

[6] Pp. 37, 42.

59

over a young man during his minority (specifically, before his marriage). It is still possible that the Yir-Yoront father, affectionate though he may be during the early years when the ethnographer contrasts his behavior with the mother's control, actually possesses in a social (not domestic) context an effective jural authority in all matters where this is of decisive importance. Homans and Schneider's inference that he does not possess such authority probably derives from their assumption that jural and affective relations will be segregated, i.e., from an assumption which such a situation as this ought precisely to test. Next, they seem to take it that there is only one kind of "respect," and that if this is reported it must denote jural authority. But this is mistaken: the Yir-Yoront mother's brother is a classificatory affine, a wife-giver to whom a debt is acknowledged, and a marked superior in this context; and the respect manifested toward him in no way entails that in addition to this he also possesses jural authority. Lastly, Homans and Schneider do not consider how the mother's brother could possibly exercise either personal discipline or recognized authority when the reference they cite says that he is continually avoided; nor, incidentally, do they relate this fact, together with the "large majority" of marriages with the mother's brother's daughter, to their argument about the influence of sentiment on rules of marriage.

In sum, the indications are that in Yir-Yoront society jural authority is not, as Homans and Schneider assert, vested in the mother's brother, and that this society is therefore not an exception to their general theory. They thus gain an unexpected point in their favor, but it is a Pyrrhic advantage.

However, such considerations aside, it still remains necessary to make a particular examination of Homans and Schneider's explanation of the matrilateral situation. To be quite clear about what we are looking for, let us set out separately some of the component propositions in their analysis:

(1) Ego is fond of his mother's brother;
(2) he will therefore visit the mother's brother often and will see a great deal of his daughter;
(3) as he is fond of the mother's brother, so he will tend to become fond of the daughter.

60

If we are to accept Homans and Schneider's theory, we have to demand in the first place clear ethnographic reports on these three propositions from at least a majority of the societies under consideration. Other propositions are also in question, of course, but these three are of first importance. It is according to the *evidence* on these three points that we must judge the account given by Homans and Schneider of how it comes about that in a patrilineal society the matrilateral rule is "adopted." What, then, is the evidence they cite?

Their response is quite extraordinary, and I therefore quote it in full. After referring to a Hehe informant who is reported to have said that a man marries his mother's brother's daughter because of his close sentimental ties with the mother's brother, they continue:

> For none of the present societies do the sources provide explicit statements of this sort. We nevertheless believe that the sentimental tie is a necessary, if not a sufficient, cause of the marriage preference, in the special sense of preceding it in time. We are in no position to demonstrate this. . . .[7]

In other words, in the plainest possible terms, Homans and Schneider offer *no* evidence in support of their general theory, absolutely none at all. Whatever are we to make of a scientific proposition put forward solely on the basis of an entirely unsupported belief on the part of its authors? I prefer to make no comment, but simply ask the reader to peruse the passage again, to appreciate its full significance.

Moreover, this kind of evidence would not help their argument in any case. As that great scholar, the lamented A. L. Kroeber, once wrote: "The completeness and plausibility of a rationalization are no index of the reality of its purported motivation; the immediacy and intensity of emotion concerning a cultural practice are no index of the origin or durability of that practice."[8] In other words, even if there did exist abundant reports of the sentiments in question, and indigenous explanations couched in terms of them, they would still not constitute evidence of a causal kind in favor of Homans and Schneider's theory.

Not only this, but for one society at least in the sample, viz.,

[7] P. 38.   [8] Kroeber, 1927, p. 313.

the Karadjeri, the evidence is there but is contrary to the argument. Marriage with the genealogical mother's brother's daughter is preferred, but there is a "taboo" on contact between a man and his mother's brother, and the wife's father is in any case avoided. Moreover, the ethnographer even explains the prohibition, among the coastal Karadjeri, on marriage with the mother's brother's daughter on the ground that "it does away with the necessity of a taboo between persons so closely bound together as mother's brother and sister's son";[9] i.e., the ground mentioned above, that a close affective relationship will not readily be converted into one of reserve. This flatly contrary evidence comes from the only source on the Karadjeri which Homans and Schneider cite.

There is also evidence on the points at issue in the ethnography on the Yaruro of Venezuela, a society not included in the sample but which should not for this reason be disregarded. The facts contradict both the special hypothesis and the general theory. The Yaruro have matrilineal moieties, and should therefore prefer marriage with the father's sister's daughter; but they actually prefer marriage with the mother's brother's daughter. "Since a boy looks to his maternal uncle for instruction and spends with him a good portion of his time, he is also coming into contact with his future wife, who should be a daughter of one of the brothers of his mother." A man has "all sorts of social obligations" toward the mother's brother, looks to him for "guidance," and has to work for him and make him presents of food. He appears to be under the authority of the mother's brother while growing up, while his father treats him with "the utmost kindness," yet marriage with the father's sister's daughter is excluded.[10] The source is unimpressive as far as social organization is concerned, and in some particulars obviously incorrect; but in it we do have evidence, exceptionally, of precisely the kind required to test Homans and Schneider's propositions—and it is utterly contradictory. Even though the jural and sentimental situation conforms to "the matrilineal complex," a man marries the matrilateral cross-cousin (i.e., contrary to the hypothesis) and to the side where authority lies (i.e., contrary to the general theory).

Natually, too, all the talk about the extension of sentiments is,

[9] Elkin, 1932, pp. 305-6.   [10] Petrullo, 1939, pp. 215-6, 219-21.

in the cases that Homans and Schneider cite, baseless. But now our authors seem to shift ground. They have explained the sentiments as the efficient causes of the adoption of the rule of marriage; and even in its most reduced form their argument is about the determinative effects of personal relations in societies as they are encountered, i.e., that the sentiments are continually "precipitated by the social structure" in such a way as to perpetuate the contraction of marriages with relatives to one side or the other. But at this point in their book they say something rather different. The sentimental tie with the mother's brother is now merely "a necessary, if not a sufficient, cause" of the marriage preference. In other words, the degree of determination is much reduced; and instead of effective causation we now appear to be seeking unknown and purely conjectured origins, without resort to actual sentiments. "We believe present association betrays ultimate origin; the history of some institutions is repeated every generation; to some unknown degree the energies that maintain a system are the ones that created it."[11] Now this is rather ingenious; for superficially it appears to lend plausibility to a purely speculative assertion about the origins and the "adoption" of rules for which there is no evidence. But of course it will not do, and our authors, with their usual honesty, admit it. "We believe this," they go on; "we do not know that we can prove it. . . ." Anyway, they say, even if this new expedient cannot be validated, "it becomes irrelevant in the face of the present association of institutions," viz., of different forms of unilateral marriage with different systems of interpersonal relations, including different loci of jural authority.

Let us pause, then, at this point to survey the position. Homans and Schneider's argument consists of two parts: (1) the establishment of an association of linearity with laterality; (2) an explanation of the association. The explanation is formally invalid, and even though it comprises the greater part of the argument and is the major point of the book, no evidence at all is presented in its favor. Moreover, evidence can be adduced which is decisively contrary. This leaves only the association of line of descent with laterality of marriage. Here at least we are on firmer and more familiar ground. What are we to make of this association?

[11] Homans and Schneider, 1955, p. 39.

III

The first point is that the nine prescriptive instances of matrilateral cross-cousin marriage—eight patrilineal, one matrilineal—prove Lévi-Strauss's structural contention. The Sirionó are matrilineal, to the point of having what would conventionally be termed a Crow terminology—and they prescribe marriage with the *matrilateral* cross-cousin.[12] It is thus empirically demonstrated that there is no necessary connection between rule of descent and laterality of prescription.

On the other hand, the Sirionó constitute a clear exception to Homans and Schneider's hypothesis, as they themselves acknowledge. But they think they can still save their general theory, on the ground that authority is patripotestal within the nuclear family.[13] A man is not under the jural authority of the mother's brother before his marriage, and to marry his daughter therefore remains sentimentally appropriate. Here we must digress for a moment to introduce and examine an additional development in Homans and Schneider's argument.

Faced with this refractory situation, they recast their hypothesis in corrected form and formulate the following proposition instead:

> Societies in which marriage is allowed or preferred with mother's brother's daughter but forbidden or disapproved with father's sister's daughter will be societies in which jural authority over ego male, before marriage, is vested in his father or father's lineage, and societies in which marriage is allowed or preferred with father's sister's daughter but forbidden or disapproved with mother's brother's daughter will be societies in which jural authority over ego male, before marriage, is vested in his mother's brother or mother's brother's lineage.[14]

As they phrase the matter later, "Potestality is a far better predictor than linearity."[15]

---

[12] Needham, 1961.   [13] P. 46.   [14] P. 51.

[15] P. 57. They precede this assertion, on the same page, with: "If anyone wants to say that we, like Lévi-Strauss, are now arguing that linearity has nothing to do with unilateral cross-cousin marriage, we shall accept the criticism, provided that he adds that we believe *potestality* has a great deal

This formulation is intended to cope with certain exceptions to the linearity-proposition which they encounter in the examination of their sample. The exceptional societies comprise two which are patrilineal-patrilateral (Kandyu, Sherente), and four which are matrilineal-matrilateral (Garo, Kaonde, Kaska, Sirionó). Before we continue with the examination of the Sirionó situation, it is instructive to direct attention to Homans and Schneider's treatment of the Sherente evidence in connection with their new formulation. They assert that "this may be a patrilineal society, but it is not a patripotestal one," "authority over ego *is not,* after an early age, vested in his father," "father is *not* the locus of jural authority over ego," and that "jural authority over ego is not vested in the father."[16] They conclude, therefore, that the Sherente actually conform to their general theory in the "negative sense" that jural authority over a boy is not, after an early age, vested where one would expect it to be in a patrilineal society.

But this is to neglect the cumulative indications of the following facts: succession to chieftainship is transmitted in the male line of a single family; parents arrange marriages of their children, disregarding their personal inclinations, and force obedience; marital residence, after the birth of a child, is taken up next to the hut of the husband's parents; a husband (i.e., a boy's father) has sole control over house and farmland; the father strikes his child as discipline in early years, and in later years is reported to inflict corporal punishment on the son for committing a serious offense; the father's brother gives an initiate his new girdle; and it is the father who gives his son his first toy weapons, decides which society he shall join and sometimes which sport team, decorates him and conducts him to the assembly place of the society, escorts him at his name-giving ceremony, and makes him his club on the occasion of his initiation.[17]

---

to do with it." Thus not only do they acknowledge a mistaken premise (see above, p. 48), and realize here that their special hypothesis is wrongly framed, but they make this astonishing *volte face* only three pages from the end of a book in which they have all along been asserting that linearity *is* a determinant. I shall not labor this point (see p. 50 above), but it bears pondering.

16 Pp. 49, 50, 57; authors' italics.

17 Nimuendajú, 1942, pp. 16, 25, 27, 31, 32, 41, 43, 46, 48, 49, 57, 81.

The mother's brother, on the other hand, apparently occupies a special position only in relation to a girl; and Homans and Schneider admit that they cannot say that authority over a boy is actually vested in him. The only evidence on which they base their repeated assertions that this is not a patripotestal society is that a boy may not join his father's association, and that in his own society he is subject to the leadership of a member of the opposite moiety. But these facts cannot reasonably be interpreted specifically as evidence regarding the locus of jural authority; and they certainly do not justify the italicized confidence of Homans and Schneider's assertions.[18] By all the signs above, this is indeed a patripotestal society; and since a man may marry his father's sister's daughter but not his maternal uncle's it thus remains an exception to Homans and Schneider's argument, including the new formulation. Potestality may well be a more useful analytical factor for their purposes than linearity, but in the case of the Sherente they have adopted a precarious means of discovering where it lies.

The question now to be taken up is whether the exceptional societies listed above are prescriptive instances. Any that are not are irrelevant to the new hypothesis as it relates to Lévi-Strauss's theory in particular and to the study of prescriptive rules of marriage in general. Of these six societies, only the Sirionó practice prescriptive unilateral cross-cousin marriage, and they are thus of singular significance in Homans and Schneider's sample in assessing the revised formulation of the hypothesis in a prescriptive context.

But the authors neglect to consider two points about the Sirionó. The first is that there is no explicit evidence specifically about the relationship with the mother's brother; so that even though we know that he does not exercise jural authority over Ego, we do not know what may be the sentimental inducements to marry his daughter. The second is that the relationship between parents-in-law and children-in-law is "the most reserved of all," and that "suppressed aggression [between them] sometimes runs high."[19] Homans and Schneider seem to permit themselves

[18] Actually they are easily interpretable by reference to the structural principle of differential complementary dualism which characterizes the whole of Sherente society, as I intend to demonstrate elsewhere. Cf. below, p. 103.

[19] Holmberg, 1950, p. 57.

to infer that because the mother's brother does not possess authority, the relationship will be close and indulgent; but this is to beg the question of the validity of the general theory. It is equally legitimate to infer (especially when, with Homans and Schneider, we assume a first-cousin marriage) that the attitude toward the mother's brother, as potential father-in-law, will be one of reserve and latent aggression.

The Sirionó evidence supports, so far as it goes, the hypothesis which was formulated to take account of it, for what significance this may have. But it is very doubtful that it agrees with the general theory; and since the new hypothesis depends on the theory, as the original linearity-hypothesis does not, any objection to the one must cast doubt on the other also. What we need, then, is a test case on which the evidence is full enough to permit a more decisive conclusion, and preferably one which the authors did not have in mind when they formulated their modified hypothesis.

This we have in an account, published some years before Homans and Schneider's book, of certain Belu of central Timor. They are matrilineal and matrilocal—and they prescribe marriage with the matrilateral cross-cousin. Children "belong" to the wife, and in the case of conflict between her family and that of her husband the latter will side with his own natal family, even to the detriment of his wife and children. It is the wife and her brother who together possess jural authority over the children, as they possess rights over land, house, hereditary property, and all other things of value. There is indeed another statement to the effect that the wife's parents are the rulers of the house, but even this does not help Homans and Schneider's theory, since on their premises the wife's father will be Ego's maternal uncle. Also, when the wife's father dies, his authority is taken over by the wife's unmarried brothers, which means that the mother's brother has at least latent authority over his sister's children.[20] The Belu evidence thus controverts the special hypothesis, the general theory, and the final formulation.

So we now have, in the prescriptive systems which are the objects of Lévi-Strauss's proposition, two exceptions to Homans and Schneider's argument. With these we are brought to the question of the significance of numbers and of statistical correlations.

[20] Vroklage, 1952, I, pp. 248–50, 265–67, 309, 410–12.

IV

The first impression created by the Belu example is that the ratio of exceptions has risen from 1:9 to 2:10, so that one-fifth of the sample is now contrary to Homans and Schneider's argument. But this is so only as long as we stick to these particular societies. If we take all the societies known to practice prescriptive matrilateral cross-cousin marriage, the number of exceptions dwindles to a proportion even more in favor of the patrilineal-matrilateral association than Homans and Schneider's cases indicate.

Here of course we encounter the familiar taxonomic difficulty of what is to count as a society, as a single instance of the rule. I do not think it is of great importance, since I do not attach much significance to numbers when trying to understand the rule of marriage in question; but something has to be said about the problem now that we have come to it. Briefly, I shall reckon as "a society" a named cultural and political grouping in which marriage is ideally or generally within the group and not with other such groups. Thus the Aimol, the Purum, and the Thado, for example, are counted as separate instances. Though belonging to the same language-family, and possessing to some degree a common culture and common social forms, they speak different languages or dialects and are distinguished from each other by many other cultural particulars, and marriages only exceptionally take place outside each society. By these criteria, I suppose the "Kachin" should be similarly subdivided, but since I am not sure what these subdivisions should be I count Kachin as one instance of the matrilateral rule. Similarly, one might distinguish a number of practically endogamous matrilateral systems on Sumba; but the published ethnography does not permit us to trace the lines between them with any certainty, and I thus count Sumba also as one instance.

By such a count there are about twenty-eight societies in the world reliably known to practice prescriptive matrilateral cross-cousin marriage. Of this figure, only three are matrilineal, while twenty-five are patrilineal. We therefore have an interesting correlation of patrilineal descent with matrilateral prescription of marriage. (The patrilineal proportion would be even higher if the Kachin and Sumbanese, both patrilineal, were subdivided.) Is this statistically very significant?

68

I tend to think that it may not be, though the answer is by no means certain. The obvious reason for doubt is the fact that there are many more patrilineal societies than matrilineal, so that given a certain number of societies with the matrilateral rule the probability might well be a proportion of patrilineal to matrilineal instances such as we have here. Homans and Schneider themselves raise this question, and they answer it by comparing the matrilineal/patrilineal ratio in Murdock's 250 societies with the ratio in their test list. In the former the figure is 0.45, in their sample it is 0.375. They therefore conclude: "We got absolutely more patrilineal societies than we had a right to expect,"[21] and they infer that they have thus not overloaded their sample with an unfair proportion of patrilineal societies. Their own figure, however, relates to their whole sample, not to the matrilateral cases with which alone we have to deal; and of course their sample is unacceptable since it is based on confused criteria. What, then, about our present total of twenty-eight prescriptive matrilateral instances? The matrilineal/patrilineal ratio among them is a mere 0.120, which in comparison with Murdock's ratio indicates once more a strong positive correlation of patrilineal descent with matrilateral prescription.

But Murdock's ratio is not that of a random sample. In fact, one of the most cogent criticisms of his *Social Structure* was that the sample was heavily biased regionally,[22] and the possibility therefore exists that there may be bias in other respects also, perhaps in favor of patrilineal societies. Similar objections attach to the ratio of 0.34 in the 331 unilineal societies in his world ethnographic sample, with respect to other non-random features of this sample. It is based primarily on a division into six "ethnographic regions," each of which is then subdivided into ten "culture areas"; so that the principle of selection is fundamentally cultural, not structural, and thus inappropriate to the decision of the present issue. Also, one example of "each major rule of descent" is included in the societies of each area, "even though there might be only a single or otherwise unimportant case." Moreover, the selection of societies is guided by a number of other specifications and negative criteria, and "duplication of es-

[21] Homans and Schneider, 1955, p. 35.

[22] Leach, 1950, p. 108.

69

sentially similar cultures" is avoided.[23] With each specification or limitation, therefore, the sample becomes less random, and the more liable to bias in one structural respect or other. The effect of these procedures on the determination of the matrilineal/patrilineal ratio is incalculable. In fact, it is practically impossible to obtain a non-random sample of societies which is of any use for the statistical testing of hypotheses.

On the other hand, a random sample would often exclude some of the fullest and most reliable accounts, and would include societies about which we often know little more than their names; so that the information on a fair proportion could not be expected to provide any useful evidence either for or against a proposition. This is the case even when we try to ascertain something so apparently simple as the ratio of matrilineal to patrilineal societies. The only solution would appear to lie, therefore, not in a random sample but in a complete enumeration. But such an investigation would soon run into all the usual difficulties of interpreting the sources—contradictory reports, unreliable accounts, and the rest—as well as, often, complete lack of information on the rule of descent. I think, therefore, that statistical procedures in the examination of this issue are not reliable or helpful.

Yet I do not want to deny that there is an interesting association of patrilineal descent with matrilateral prescription in the figures as they stand. What I want to emphasize is (1) the taxonomic difficulty in deciding what shall count as a single instance of a matrilateral system, a decision which determines the result of any statistical analysis; and (2) the absence of a certain criterion for determining the degree to which the matrilineal/patrilineal ratio may be disproportionate with a random expectation. I would tend to agree that there probably is a patrilineal-matrilateral association, but I think it impossible to make any exact or useful statistical assertions about it.

How this association is to be interpreted, though, is another matter. I trust that it will be clear by now that neither Homans and Schneider's general theory nor their special hypothesis helps us to understand the apparently disproportionate predominance of patrilineal instances. But Lévi-Strauss does suggest a possible answer (though admittedly with respect to the particular and incorrect correlation which Homans and Schneider propose). If a

[23] Murdock, 1957, pp. 666–67, 687.

significant statistical correlation exists, he says, the explanation probably lies in the instability peculiar to matrilineal societies, which makes it more difficult for them to adopt the "long cycle" of indirect exchange.[24] He does not elaborate the point, and I do not think it appropriate that I should try to make his argument for him; but it has an immediate structural plausibility, and there is also revealing factual evidence from an existing matrilineal-matrilateral society which supports it.

The matrilineal Belu mentioned above do indeed manifest the strains and instability of which Lévi-Strauss writes. We have seen some of the evidence already, and it is only necessary to add certain further indications. A man works in his wife's family, but "belongs" to and aligns himself with his own. He works under the authority of his wife's family, and with property belonging to that family; he raises crops on the land belonging to it, and has to hand over the produce and proceeds of sales to his wife and her brother. In common speech the wife is known as the "mistress of the house," a position of which she is very conscious, and this is the source of frequent dissension. The ethnographer says that this allocation of rights (including rights over children) cannot be too highly stressed, and reports that "it causes a deep rift in the marriage relationship and is a strong hindrance to the organic unity of the family."[25]

Here then are instabilities of the kind to which Lévi-Strauss refers, and they occur in this instance of matrilateral alliance because the society is matrilineal and matrilocal. They do not, on the other hand, typically or usually appear in matrilateral alliance systems which are patrilineal and patrilocal, nor do such systems manifest any comparable features. Since the solidary characteristics of a matrilateral system must depend on the strength of the particular links which compose the alliances between groups, obviously these weaknesses and instabilities entail a lesser degree of "organic solidarity" in an alliance system of this sort. In other words, a matrilineal-matrilocal system is subject to structural weaknesses and works less well than a patrilineal-patrilocal system: i.e., it is a less solidary arrangement. The existential ramifications of this characteristic will become clear later when we have looked at how a matrilateral alliance system really works.

[24] Lévi-Strauss, 1958, p. 344.   [25] Vroklage, 1952, I, p. 411.

Finally, I come to a far weightier point of method. One of Homans and Schneider's charges against Lévi-Strauss, to which they ascribe his supposed failure to see the correct explanation of unilateral cross-cousin marriage, is that "his model of social behavior is too formal and abstract."[26] But what about their own? How adequately does it represent the complexities of the types of social system to which their argument should apply?

They concentrate on linearity, and this is consonant with their psychological interest in the sentiments associated with the allocation of authority in lineal descent systems. But is it so sure that linearity alone is the analytically significant factor (or, as they misleadingly put it, the "determinant")? They themselves have to concede at one point that the marriage "preference" may persist for such a time as to "become an established norm and linked with aspects of social organization other than the sentimental tie," e.g., with the transmission of bridewealth.[27] But why stop there? How is one to know what may or may not be the important features for the explanation of unilateral cross-cousin marriage? Clearly, not by elementary statistical correlations in terms of only four variables, nor by superficial comparison of any other kind.

The point that I wish to make, with all possible force, is this. You cannot compare, or attempt to explain, what you do not first understand. Now it is quite remarkable that Homans and Schneider do not analyze in detail any one single society of the prescriptive type to which they suppose their argument to apply, and show no sign of having done so. Nor, to judge by the references they make, have they even examined all the published evidence on any one of the prescriptive societies they deal with. Not only this, but other scholars have worked on these problems, yet our authors make no reference to views other than those which they attribute to Lévi-Strauss. In other words, they have neglected the evidence, and they do not understand the object of their study.

The ethnographic evidence so far referred to presents us with only matrilateral cases, yet it is clear from their declared premises that Homans and Schneider have radically misconceived the constitution and operation of a society with a matrilateral prescrip-

[26] Homans and Schneider, 1955, p. 59.

[27] P. 39.

tive marriage system, the values by which it is inspired, and the principles by which it is governed.

The way to acquire such an understanding is by a total structural analysis of all the recorded facts on one society. This means surveying every facet of social life, not merely the allocation of authority within a narrow circle of domestic relatives, or even the conventional institutions of "kinship" and marriage. Such an examination involves a systematic comprehension of the life of a society in terms of the classification employed by the people themselves, and an analysis in terms of relations of the widest generality. It is not until such an investigation has been completed that it is possible to frame any useful questions about the type of system to which that society belongs, let alone to ask why it is what it is and not something different.

Chapter Four

No theory is likely to endure which does
not arise directly out of long-continued, in-
tuitive familiarity with the welter of facts
which it attempts to order.—HOMANS[1]

ANALYSIS

Let us now examine the main features of one society with a
matrilateral prescription. This will be the Purum of the Indo-
Burma border. It has to be admitted that the ethnographic rec-
ords on this society are not in all respects as comprehensive or reliable as the information available on other societies of the same
type, but I choose this society because in certain particulars the
ethnography is the most useful for testing Homans and Schneider's argument.

The following account is based on a more extended analysis already published, and therefore includes without further discussion points which I think I have already demonstrated. It also
includes certain material which for one reason or another was
omitted from the original paper.[2] The bulk of the information
comes from the monograph by Das.[3]

I

The Purum are an "Old Kuki" tribe of Manipur, on the eastern border of India. They are of Mongoloid physical stock, and
speak a Tibeto-Burman language. In 1932, i.e., in the period from
which our information mostly comes, they numbered 303 individuals. They are divided among four villages: there are no non-
Purum in these villages, and there are no Purum in other villages. Marriage is permissible with the Chawte, another Old

[1] Homans, 1942, p. 402.

[2] Needham, 1958*a*. A complete analysis, argued without consideration of
length and very much amplified, will appear in a future monograph. For
another analysis of the same kind, relating to a different culture, see Needham, 1960*c*.

[3] Das, 1945.

Kuki tribe with whom the Purum claim a common historical origin, but no cases are reported.

The villages are politically autonomous, each governed by its own council. There is no indigenous centralized government or judiciary. The villages are linked, however, in the first place, by the fact that every clan except one (and this also in the past) is represented in every village. We cannot assert on the evidence available that the villages are related to each other as villages on this basis; but local descent groups in different villages are related

TABLE 3

PURUM DESCENT GROUPS

| | | VILLAGE | | |
CLAN	LINEAGE	Khulen (Kh)	Tampak (Ta)	Chumbang (Chu)
Kheyang (K)......	1. Julhung	+	+	+
	2. Aihung	....	+	+
Makan (Mk)......	1. Kankung	+	+	+
	2. Makan-te	+	....	....
Marrim (M).......	1. Rimphunchong	+	....	....
	2. Rimkung	+	....	....
	3. Rim-ke-lek	....	+	....
	4. Pilling	....	+	+
Parpa (P).........	....	+	+	+
Thao (T).........	1. Thao-kung	....	+	....
	2. Thao-run	+	....	....
	3. Teyu	....	....	....
	4. Rangshai	+	....	....

by common clanship, and since the component groups are so related it may well be that the villages are politically related also within the descent system.

There are five named, exogamous patrilineal clans, which are further distinguished by personal names traditionally proper to each clan, and by possessing separate sections within each village burial ground. Four of the clans are subdivided into named lineages. The names of these descent groups, and their distribution throughout the three villages for which such information is available, are shown in Table 3. Mnemonic letters are appended to the names of the clans and villages, and the lineages are numbered; so that in the following analysis M_3, for example, will stand for Rim-ke-lek lineage of Marrim clan. One lineage of Thao clan

75

(viz., Teyu) died out in 1924, but is retained in the table because it has a place in the argument.

The descent groups are systematically related by ties of prescriptive alliance. The prescribed marriage is with the "mother's brother's daughter," while marriage with the "father's sister's daughter" is strictly forbidden. The rule, however, does not enjoin marriage with the individual matrilateral first cousin, but also covers marriage with a woman from the clan of the mother's brother, i.e., with a woman who does not stand in any particular

TABLE 4

PURUM CATEGORIES OF DESCENT AND ALLIANCE

f.	m.	← f.	m.	← f.	m.	← f.
			pu	pi	pu	pi
	rang	ni	pa	nu	pu	pi
tu	tu	u sar nau	ta [ego] nau	nau	pu	pi
tu	tu	sha	sha	nau mau	pu	
tu	tu	tu	tu			

degree of genealogical relationship. The actual marriage is contracted by a three-year period of bride-service, after which residence is patrilocal.

The relationship terminology (see also Table 4) accords with the rule of descent and with the marriage prescription:[4]

[4] It may prove interesting to keep the following observation in mind during the course of this chapter: "A disproportionate amount of attention has been given to kinship terminology, largely because it includes the facts about kinship that are most easily collected. . . . We shall not discuss the different systems of kinship terminology, suspecting that systems which look rather unlike one another may be so because, in effect, a close decision went one way rather than another" (Homans, 1951, p. 223). There could hardly be a remark more revealing of the bias which inspires *Marriage, Authority, and Final Causes,* or so indicative of the roots of its failure.

1. *pu*	FF,MF,MB,WF,MBS,WB,WBS	
2. *pi*	FM,MM,MBW,WM,WBW	
3. *pa*	F,FB,MZH	
4. *nu*	M,MZ,FBW	
5. *ni*	FZ	
6. *rang*	FZH	
7. *ta*	eB,FBSe,MZSe	
8. *u*	eZ,FBDe,MZDe	
9. *nau*	yB,FBSy,MZSy,yZ,MZDy,MBD,BW,WBD	
10. *sar*	Z	
11. *mau*	SW.	
12. *sha*	S,BS,WZS,D,BD,WZD	
13. *tu*	FZS,ZH,FZD,ZS,DH,ZD,SS,SD,	
	DSW,DS,SDH,DD.	

The equations and distinctions are characteristic. The following, among others, confirm that we are dealing with a lineal descent system:

F = FB	FB ≠ MB
M = MZ	FZ ≠ MZ
B = FBS	B ≠ MBS
S = BS	B ≠ FZS
	S ≠ WBS
	S ≠ ZS

And these demonstrate the matrilateral prescription:

FB = MZH	FZ ≠ MBW
MB = WF	FZH ≠ WF
MBS = WB	MBD ≠ FZD
MBD = BW	WB ≠ ZH
B = MZS, WZH	WBW ≠ Z
FZS = ZH	WBS ≠ ZS
ZS = DH	SW ≠ ZD
S = WZS	
DS = SDH	

The only point to occasion misgiving is the equation of mother's brother's daughter with younger sister, which is utterly uncharacteristic of such systems as this.[5] It is understandable that

[5] The related Chawte, who may have the same marriage prescription, are reported to make the same equation; but the ethnography on this society is quite unreliable in such respects (Needham, 1960*a*).

the term may denote brother's wife, and wife's sister after her marriage, for these women may well be addressed by the same terms as are the men to whom they are married, and especially since a woman is incorporated into her husband's group; but there is no ready explanation for this infraction of one of the cardinal rules of matrilateral terminologies, viz., that marriageable women must be distinguished from prohibited women. Yet the ethnographer so clearly and repeatedly gives the particular term for the matrilateral cross-cousin that we may not easily doubt his report. However, another source gives *sar* for "sister," a term common in other Kuki languages, and by this at least the sister is clearly distinguished from the mother's brother's daughter. Also it is only the younger sister who is not so distinguished, while the elder is known by a term (*u*) which is not reported as applicable to the mother's brother's daughter.

The relationships of affinity are not merely ties between individuals or families. Descent groups, whether localized or dispersed, are also related as groups by ties of prescriptive alliance. A descent group may take wives by traditional claim from certain groups but not from others; women are transferred obligatorily in one "direction," and there can be no direct exchange. The total society is divided by the Purum themselves into: (1) lineally related descent groups, (2) wife-giving groups, (3) wife-taking groups; and the fundamental cycle of alliance is exhibited by the specific statement that a wife-taking group may be identical with a wife-giving group of one's own wife-givers (see Fig. 1).

Members of these three major categories, each of which may comprise one or more descent groups in relation to any particular descent group, are terminologically related in the same way as individuals are related in particular affinal relationships. All the men of a wife-giving group are *pu,* a term of which one of the genealogical specifications is "mother's brother"; and all the men of Ego's generation and below in a wife-taking group are *tu,* one of the specifications of which is "sister's son." Within Ego's own generation all the women of any wife-giving group are *nau(nu),* one of the genealogical specifications of which is "mother's brother's daughter"; and all those of a wife-taking group are *tu(nu),* one of the specifications of which is "father's sister's daughter."

Purum society thus exhibits the structural categories and relations of a social system based on prescribed marriage with the "mother's brother's daughter." We may now examine the individual marriages which actually take place and which maintain this system. The information is perfectly clear on the vital point that marriage is not necessarily or even usually with the matrilateral first cousin, but with a classificatory matrilateral cross-cousin. Analysis of the 54 marriages recorded from three villages (Khulen, Tampak, and Changninglong) shows that no fewer than 26 (48.1 per cent) are with women of clans other than that of the mother (Table 5). This means that at least this proportion of marriages in this record could not possibly have been with the daughter of the maternal uncle. Furthermore, the proportion is

TABLE 5
MARRIAGES OUTSIDE THE MOTHER'S CLAN

		Clan of Wife					Total	Outside Mother's Clan
		K	Mk	M	P	T		
Clan of Mother	K....	3	....	....	....	2	5	2
	Mk...	....	3	....	1	....	4	1
	M....	6	....	6	2	....	14	8
	P....	....	5	2	5	3	15	10
	T....	....	1	2	2	11	16	5
Total......		....	....	....	....	....	54	26

cetainly higher, for it is not possible to distinguish in the evidence marriages with the first cousin from marriages with a classificatory relative of the same category in the mother's clan.

This single fact is of the gravest consequence, as we shall see even more clearly later, for Homans and Schneider's theory. Their argument applies specifically and exclusively to marriage with the first cousin. It is conceivable that a theory of sentiments might help to elucidate marriage with such a close relative; but it is not readily conceivable how it could possibly apply to a situation in which nearly half the women married come from clans other than that of the mother. How could it ever be thought likely that marriages with all such women should be "sentimentally appropriate" in the way proposed by Homans and Schneider?

Before we expatiate on this point, let us proceed to an examination of the relations between groups established and maintained by such marriages. In Table 6 is presented a scheme of alliances between all the component descent groups of Purum society. The groups of reference constitute the center column; the arrows show the direction of transfer of women. Wife-givers are on the left, wife-takers on the right; so that, e.g., K_1 takes wives from Mk_2, from M_2, etc., and gives wives to Mk_1, to M_1, and to M_3. What does this mean in terms of Homans and Schneider's theory? For any man in K_1, every woman in his own genealogical level in every one of the wife-giving groups, viz., Mk_2, M_2, M_4, P, T_1, T_2, T_3, and T_4 is a "mother's brother's daughter." Further-

TABLE 6

SCHEME OF ALLIANCES

$$Mk_2, M_2, M_4, P, T_1, T_2, T_3, T_4 \rightarrow \quad K_1 \rightarrow Mk_1, M_1, M_3$$
$$Mk_1, Mk_2, M_2, P, T_1, T_4 \rightarrow \quad K_2 \rightarrow M_1, M_3, M_4$$
$$K_1, M_2, P \rightarrow Mk_1 \rightarrow K_2, M_1, M_3, M_4, T_1, T_2, T_3, T_4$$
$$K_1, M_1, M_2, M_3, M_4, P \rightarrow Mk_2 \rightarrow K_2, T_1, T_2, T_3, T_4$$
$$K_1, K_2, Mk_1 \rightarrow \quad M_1 \rightarrow Mk_2, P$$
$$T_1, T_2, T_3 \rightarrow \quad M_2 \rightarrow K_1, K_2, Mk_1, Mk_2, P$$
$$K_1, K_2, Mk_1, T_1, T_2, T_3, T_4 \rightarrow \quad M_3 \rightarrow Mk_2, P$$
$$K_2, Mk_1, T_1, T_2, T_3 \rightarrow \quad M_4 \rightarrow K_1, Mk_2, P$$
$$M_1, M_2, M_3, M_4 \rightarrow \quad P \rightarrow K_1, K_2, Mk_1, Mk_2, T_1, T_2$$
$$Mk_1, Mk_2, P \rightarrow \quad T_1 \rightarrow K_1, K_2, M_2, M_3, M_4$$
$$Mk_1, Mk_2, P \rightarrow \quad T_2 \rightarrow K_1, M_2, M_3, M_4$$
$$Mk_1, Mk_2 \rightarrow \quad T_3 \rightarrow K_1, M_2, M_3, M_4$$
$$Mk_1, Mk_2 \rightarrow \quad T_4 \rightarrow K_1, K_2, M_3$$

more, each of these alliance groups may comprise a number of local alliance groups: e.g., the local representatives of Parpa clan in the three villages of Khulen, Tampak, and Changninglong.

If a man is going to visit "the mother's brother" often, as Homans and Schneider say he does, he is going to do an awful lot of walking. But why ever should he? Because, Homans and Schneider tell us, he is "fond" of the mother's brother. To be fond of roughly a third of all the men of his father's generation in the total society seems a promiscuous lavishing of sentiment, but suppose he is? Well, then, we are told, "he will tend to get fond of the daughter." But this, similarly, means being fond of something like one-third of all the women in his own generation, a very expansive affection. Anyway, he is held to have a "sentimental claim" to all these young women, marriage with any one of this large class will be "sentimentally appropriate"—and this implausible tale is the real explanation of the rule of marriage.

The facts so far examined are damaging enough to Homans and Schneider's argument, but we have hardly begun to see the complexity of the social and symbolic systems associated with the rule of marriage. It will be recalled that a defining feature of a system with a matrilateral prescription is the "cycle" of women linking the descent groups into a system, the *"échange généralisé"* of Lévi-Strauss. In the model this is a single cycle (Fig. 1); but, as we should expect, the factual situation which this so simply represents is very much more complex. From Table 6 we can

TABLE 7

Examples of Alliance Cycles

1. K_1—M_1—Mk_2—K_2—M_3—P—(K_1)
2. K_1—M_1—Mk_2—K_2—M_4—(K_1)
3. K_1—M_1—Mk_2—K_2—M_4—P—(K_1)
4. K_1—M_1—Mk_2—T_1—(K_1)
5. K_1—M_3—Mk_2—K_2—M_1—P—(K_1)
6. K_1—M_3—Mk_2—K_2—M_4—(K_1)
7. K_1—M_3—Mk_2—T_1—(K_1)
8. K_1—Mk_1—M_1—Mk_2—K_2—M_3—P—(K_1)
9. K_1—Mk_1—M_1—P—(K_1)
10. K_1—Mk_1—M_1—Mk_2—K_2—M_3—P—(K_1)
11. K_1—Mk_1—M_1—Mk_2—T_1—(K_1)
12. K_1—Mk_1—M_3—P—(K_1)
13. K_1—Mk_1—M_4—(K_1)
14. K_1—Mk_2—T_1—(K_1)
15. K_2—M_1—Mk_2—(K_2)
16. K_2—M_1—P—(K_2)
17. M_1—P—Mk_1—(M_1)
18. M_2—Mk_1—T_1—(M_2)
19. M_2—Mk_2—T_1—(M_2)
20. M_3—P—Mk_1—(M_3)

determine what degree of correspondence there is between the features of the model and those of social reality. There are a large number of cycles to be discerned in it, of which Table 7 gives twenty examples. There are many others to be extracted from the scheme of alliances, but these are ample to show the large number and the complexity of the affinal ties linking a small number of intermarrying descent groups. Complex though this representation is, it is nevertheless an abstraction from a still more complex reality in terms of local groups. The relation K_1–Mk_1 is a simple relationship between two distinct, named descent groups; but it has to be remembered—if we are to appreciate more exactly what happens in terms of people on the ground—that K_1 comprises three local descent groups, one in each of the villages in Table 3, and that Mk1 also comprises three territorially separate groups. An analysis of alliance cycles as they in fact link such local groups—which is what a political study of Purum society would ultimately involve—would therefore be far more complex than the situation as I have analyzed it here. In fact, the further we go into the evidence, the more complex in its particulars a social system based on a matrilateral prescription is seen to be—and the more inapt Homans and Schneider's explanation of it.

The reference to a political study brings us finally to the relationships established between villages by the alliances between their component local descent groups. These can be seen from

TABLE 8

INTERVILLAGE MARRIAGES

		MARRIED INTO			TOTAL MARRIAGES	WOMEN MARRIED OUT OF VILLAGE
	→	Kh	Ta	Cha		
WOMEN FROM	Kh.....	30	3	1	34	4
	Ta......	6	10	......	16	6
	Cha.....	1	......	3	4	1
Total........		......	......	......	54	11

Table 8. Out of the fifty-four marriages recorded, eleven (20.3 per cent) have taken place between villages. That is, the autonomous political units of Purum society are also related by the alliances between descent groups which are fundamental to social life.

In sum, so far as the social order is concerned, the same tripartite categorization orders relations between individuals, between descent groups, and between the component local descent groups of the village, and creates ties between the politically independent villages.

II

At this point, let us return to the confrontation of Homans and Schneider's theory with the facts. Here we have a patrilineal society, with patrilocal residence; inheritance and succession are

82

through males exclusively; it is local groups of men who constitute the social and political segments of Purum society between which women are transferred. These groups are allied in the first place by the matrilateral prescription, and their members are denoted by terms which are not genealogically defined designations but are categories defined by descent and alliance.

It should be noted especially that structurally this social classification is exactly congruent with the system diagramed in Homans and Schneider's Figure 1, save for the fact (which we may now recognize as formally irrelevant) that the Purum system is patrilineal while their figure is matrilineal. More particularly, all the positional equations and distinctions which have been elicited from the Purum terminology are present in Homans and Schneider's diagram also. This diagram is their representation of a system of "matrilateral cross-cousin marriage," in terms of which their argument is premised and to which their theory is intended (however partially or confusedly) to apply. Purum society, then, is precisely a patrilineal instance of this type of system. The only reservation to be registered is that, while the Purum are indeed patripotestal, we are not told what are the sentiments toward the father's sister and the mother's brother, and we therefore do not know whether this is sentimentally a typical instance of Homans and Schneider's "patrilineal complex." The probability is that the Purum configuration of attitudes does conform, but we do not know this for certain. Nor do we know what are the sentiments toward the father's sister's daughter and the mother's brother's daughter. In all other respects, however, Purum ethnography provides an eminently satisfactory case for the empirical testing of Homans and Schneider's theory in its application to matrilateral prescriptive systems. Now this society is patrilineal and its prescription is matrilateral, and it thus supports the correlation in the special hypothesis; but this is not now a very significant issue. What we have constantly to bear in mind in the course of this analysis is the question of whether it is likely that this system may be understood by reference to the sentiments from which, according to Homans and Schneider, the rules of marriage derive.

There are two kinds of relations fundamental to this type of society: (1) between lineally related men; (2) between affines. The corporate group is the lineal descent group, and within it its members are differentiated terminologically according to generation, relative age, and sex; and this is consistent with the differentiation of status normally found essential to the conduct of social life by such a group. On the other hand, the lineal descent group is flanked, as it were, by other such groups with which it is related by alliance—its affines; and, with the exception of one position (viz., *rang*), these groups are not internally differentiated in relation to it. There are *pu*-lines and there are *tu*-lines. These categories include men under one status regardless of their individual attributes of age, genealogical level, rank, or cognatic connection. An alliance group denoted by *pu* is one from which wives are obtained: it is a wife-giving group. An alliance group denoted by *tu* is one to which wives are given: it is a wife-taking group, and marriage with its women is forbidden. Paradigmatically, the second of the two basic kinds of relation, that of alliance, is *pu-tu*.

Now let us look more closely at the connotations of these terms. Wife-givers are denoted by a term (*pu*) which applies also to senior lineal kinsmen; wife-takers are denoted by a term (*tu*) which applies also to the most junior lineal kin (see Table 4). These terms in themselves indicate that there is a differentiation of status between affines, and here we approach the content of what so far have been dealt with simply as formal relations. In systems of matrilateral prescriptive alliance it is commonly the case that wife-givers are regarded as superior to wife-takers. The probability now appears that this is the case among the Purum also, and we shall see this confirmed later.

Now, then: the category of woman with whom marriage is prescribed is essentially a daughter or sister of any man (a *pu*) in a wife-giving group. Among these alliance groups there is one to which Ego's mother belonged; within it there is one local alliance group from which she came; and within that group one of the number of men denoted by the term *pu* is the maternal uncle. It is on the basis of this slender circumstance that observers have tended to report that marriage is with the "mother's brother's daughter."

But this particular individual is only one of a large proportion of maritally eligible women belonging to different descent groups, and dispersed over a number of local alliance groups. Similar considerations apply also to the men and women denoted by *tu,* and particularly to the genealogically defined "father's sister's daughter." But these two categories of women are defined, not by genealogical connection but by alliance. It is inaccurate and misleading even to call them the "matrilateral cross-cousin" and "patrilateral cross-cousin." These terms are constructed from the point of view of an individual in a junior generation, whereas alliances are contracted (as is usually the case, and as we shall see is so among the Purum) by members of the senior generation. The relationship contracted is between men in positions to whose definition terms relating to "mother" and "father" are not necessarily relevant. And even from the point of view of Ego in the junior generation, the "matrilateral" cross-cousin whom he marries may well have no connection with his own mother except a terminological one. She may come, that is, from a different descent group (e.g., clan), a different alliance group, a different local alliance group, and a different political and territorial group. Similar considerations apply to the "patrilateral" cross-cousin and to the relation of Ego's father to persons denoted by the term *tu*.

Finally, I wish to emphasize a point which is of quite radical importance, to my mind the most important in this book, viz., that since these categories are those by which other people order their social lives, it is essential when examining a system of prescriptive alliance first of all to make the most intense imaginative effort to think in terms of their classification. This is basically what I mean by "understanding"; but no valid understanding, by contrast, is ever likely to result from genealogical definitions of status, from a purview confined to domestic relationships, or from the pernicious theory of the extension of sentiments.

These considerations bring us back to Homans and Schneider and to the comparison of their argument with the facts as I have presented them. Let me first draw attention to one vital analytical fact, viz., that in this summing-up I started with a consideration of the society as a whole, in factual terms of groups of men; then isolated the fundamental relations which unite these groups into a society; and only gradually particularized to the final point at which individuals were distinguished. This I take to be the characteristic procedure of the social anthropologist. Homans and Schneider, on the contrary, deal with the individual and with his sentimental reactions to other individuals within an extremely narrowly defined family situation; and this approach is determined by the nature of their interest, which is not sociological but psychological. This would not matter, of course, if only it helped us to understand this kind of society. But, far from this being the case, Purum society cannot even be described by the terms and relations of their model. It is not simply that they do not go any further in the analysis of a matrilateral system: from their premises, they cannot.

There is one expedient by which they might try to save their argument, but it is a desperate one. This is by an extreme application of the extension theory. The sentiment associated with the mother's brother, it might be contended, is extended to other men of his local descent group; thence to the men of this generation in all the component groups of his descent group; and thence to such men in all the descent groups which stand in the same alliance relationship to Ego's as that to which his maternal uncle belongs. One would hope, of course, that no social anthropologist today would seriously advance such an argument; but it might just possibly be held that in this process lies the validation of the theory of sentiments. In that case, though, the new formulation would run even more disastrously into the difficulties in the extension theory which we examined in chapter 2, and I need not rehearse these. Moreover, we have now seen a hint of yet one more difficulty, viz., that the mother's brother is a member of a superior category (the point may be conceded for the moment: it will be borne out below), and that the conventional attitude towards members of this category in general is likely to be one of respect and distance, not of the affectionate intimacy that the theory demands.

But, all this aside, there is in any case the main question: What would be the analytical advantage in adopting the argument from sentiments? It certainly cannot offer a better understanding of the social classification than that to be gained by apprehending the classification through its own categories and principles; it is irrelevant to the significance of the sociological analysis made so far; and there is no evidence in the ethnography to allow us to believe that it isolates the efficient causes of the "adoption" or maintenance of the marriage rule which defines the social system.

Finally, one more particular point on which Homans and Schneider's theory diverges ruinously from the facts. They maintain that Lévi-Strauss "neglects the degree to which natives depart from the norm in practice, and depart from it they must."[6] One example of such departure, they think, is when a classificatory cross-cousin is married, and the evidence just examined shows that this is quite wrong. But it could still be the case that, for one reason or another, difficulty arises in marrying a woman of the correct category. Must there then be "departure from the norm"? Will a man have to marry a woman of the category of *tu*? The answer, to judge by the common practice in other such societies and particularly by a report from the related Chawte, is that he will not. What typically happens is that a woman is removed from a normally non-marriageable category and adopted into a marriageable one.[7] Her genealogical connection—e.g., as father's sister's daughter—is entirely disregarded, and she is ritually assigned to the appropriate category in the classification which in fact orders social life. This expedient in itself demonstrates the paramountcy of the classification over the factors of genealogy and individual sentiment to which Homans and Schneider mistakenly attribute such determinative importance.

So much for the main features of the social order, and particularly the descent system and the regulation of marriage to which Homans and Schneider's argument is intended to apply. I now turn to a brief consideration of the symbolic order, where their theory encounters yet more deleterious and invalidating difficulties.

III

Whatever its analytical and empirical complications, a society based on matrilateral alliance is fundamentally a very simple and clearly defined system. It is therefore the more feasible to determine, through a consideration of its symbolic usages, whether or not there are more abstract structural principles underlying both social relations of the sorts we have examined above and other aspects of its culture which are not obviously connected with them. What we seek is in fact (so far as the literature allows) the "total structure" of Purum society. The ethnography on this particular instance of the system is not the most revealing in this respect, but it is possible to glimpse, chiefly in the symbolism of

[6] Homans and Schneider, 1955, p. 6.

[7] Needham, 1960*b*.

ritual, certain structural features which are radical to Purum society.

A convenient and characteristic point at which to start is the house and its divisions (Fig. 5). This is divided lengthwise into two named parts: *phumlil* on the right (looking from a position inside at the back) and *ningan* on the left. The "master of the house" has his bed in the *phumlil* half, near a special post called *chhatra*, and his unmarried sons and daughters sleep near him on

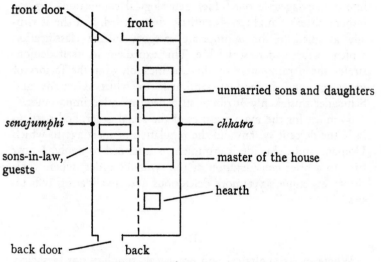

NINGAN   PHUMLIL

front door

front

unmarried sons and daughters

senajumphi —   *chhatra*

sons-in-law, guests

master of the house

hearth

back door —   back

FIG. 5.—Plan of Purum house. (After Das, 1945, Plate XIX, Fig. 74.)

the same side. Future sons-in-law (men who live in the house while fulfilling their bride-service) and other young men who pass the nights there as guests (courting the unmarried daughters) sleep in the *ningan* half, near a post called *senajumphi*. At night the *phumlil* is taboo to those outsiders who sleep in the *ningan*, and even married daughters of the house sleep in the *ningan* when they visit their parents' home. The two posts *chhatra* and *senajumphi*, associated respectively with *phumlil* and *ningan*, are of ritual importance. When the house is built they are erected in a fixed order: first *chhatra*, then *senajumphi*; and the stringers which rest on them are also put up in the same order. This order, this ascription of primacy, seems to accord with a difference in status which evidently exists between the two sides of the house, for without doubt the master of the house is of superior status to the sons-in-law who labor for him and to casual young guests. *Phumlil,* we may infer, is superior to *ningan,* and *chhatra* is superior to *senajumphi.* The front door is in what I have designated the "left" (*ningan*) side of the house, and so is the back door. These facts may also be regarded as consistent with the inferred inferior character of this side of the house. The hearth, on the other hand, is in *phumlil:* we know what importance this usually possesses, and we shall see that it is ritually important among the Purum. We may see in this sum of conventional dispositions a division of the house into private and public, family and outsiders, kin and affines, all subsumed under the general characters of superior (*phumlil*) and inferior (*ningan*). Related to this scheme is the probability that the back is superior to the front of the house. In the same way as the stringers are placed right (*phumlil*) first, left (*ningan*) second, so the crossbeam at the back is traditionally set in place first and then the crossbeam at the front. This in turn is consistent with the facts that the house-owner's bed, the hearth, and the altar of the house-god are all in the back part of the house. These circumstances also confirm the ascription of the designations "right" and "left."

Another context in which the opposition of right and left is seen is the sacrifice of a fowl to the god of the house or the clan. The position of the legs of the bird at the time of death augurs the future of the sacrificers: if the right leg is on top of the left, it augurs well; but if the left is on top of the right it augurs ill. Here, then, right is auspicious, left inauspicious: i.e., right is superior to left. I think it is significant, too, that a sacrificial animal (pig or buffalo) is speared in the right side. This differentiation of value is confirmed by another situation, which clinches the argument with a further correlation. At the name-giving ceremony for a child of either sex, augury is sought in the same way in order to ascertain the child's future. In the case of a boy, a cock is strangled by the priest; and here also if the right is on top of the left leg it is regarded as a good omen, while the reverse forebodes evil. This we readily understand, but now the ritual opposition of right and left is reversed, in a feminine context. In the case of a girl, the ceremony is performed with a hen; and it is if the left leg is on top of the right that the augury is good, while the right on the left forebodes ill. We need not be surprised at this contextual reversal of the symbolism of the legs, nor does it controvert the inference about the general significance of right and left. As we shall see later, it introduces a scheme of oppositions wider than the opposition of the sides, and with which this particular instance of differential interpretation is entirely consistent. The interesting matter at this point is that male is associated with right and female with left.

This brings us back to the divisions of the house. Now *phumlil* is the "masculine" side, associated with the master of the house and with the resident males who are stationary while the women circulate. *Ningan* is certainly the "feminine" side, for the word also denotes all the women of the house, without distinction of generation, after they have been married out of the family and their clan. That is, it denotes women who have been transferred to wife-taking groups. Significantly, as we have seen, daughters who have married out sleep in the *ningan* half when they visit their parents, not in the *phumlil;* so that their status in the alliance system is marked even by the place where they have now to sleep in the house where they were born. This confirms, too, the association of kin with the *phumlil* side, affines with the *ningan* side of the house.

We may now introduce the term *maksa,* which most prominently denotes the husbands of the father's sister, the sister, and the daughter. There is of course the distinct term *rang* for father's sister's husband, while males of the succeeding generations are in any case denoted by the one term *tu;* but the term *maksa* is evidently not redundant. It denotes, not simply members of wife-taking categories, but individual men with whom alliances (by the cession of women to them) have actually been contracted.

The *maksa* are of supreme social and ritual importance to their wife-givers. At a certain prestige-feast it is the *maksa* of the celebrant who ceremonially kills the ox on his behalf, spearing it (significantly) in the right side. At the agricultural festival of Shanghong, each of the village officials performs a rite in connection with the rice and provides rice beer for the villagers; and it is the *maksa* who prepares the beer. At the installation feast of a village official, it is his *maksa* who distributes the rice beer. It is the *maksa* who is in charge of building a new house, not the house-owner; who prepares the rice beer for the feast of formal entry; who ceremonially kindles the first fire in it (cf. the observation above on the symbolic importance of the hearth); and who kills the animals for the feast.

An important ceremony in a child's life—that, in fact, at which his social life begins—is the first hair-cutting, by which he is ritually separated from the ancestral spirits and brought into membership of the lineage group. Rice beer and curried pork are offered to the ancestors, and it is the *maksa* and the *ningan* (their wives) who prepare the offerings. A pig is killed by the *maksa* and is then placed on the veranda with its head pointing east. Not only is the beer made by the *ningan,* but they must fetch the water for it themselves. This means that a *ningan* cannot be helped by women of her natal clan, for whose members the beer is made and to whose ancestors it is offered. The stipulation marks ritually the wife's complete severance from her natal group—she is so assimilated into her husband's group that when she dies she is buried in the cemetery of his clan—and maintains the symbolic separation of the alliance groups. At the feast the *maksa* and *ningan* sit apart from the elders and adult men of the child's descent group, with the young men, women, and children.

At the end of the period of bride-service it is the *maksa* who go to the house of the groom's father, kill a pig provided by him, and prepare a special sort of curry. This they take to the bride's house, with *ningan* bearing containers of rice beer. This party which goes out to bring back the married couple, to transfer the woman physically and finally from her natal group into that with which her marriage creates an alliance, consists of only *maksa* and *ningan* of the husband's group. No member of the clan of the groom's father can go, or can share the presents of meat and beer made at the feast in the house of the bride's father. These items are taboo to the bride and groom themselves, and to all female members who belong by birth to the bride's clan. The *maksa* and *ningan* bring the wife to the house of her husband's father.

At a burial the *maksa* are equally important. They wash the body of their "wife's father," and dress it; one of them spears a pig, and they prepare rice beer. The *ningan* may also bring rice beer with them: this is drunk by the village officials and other guests, but rice beer and other comestibles belonging to the house of the deceased cannot be touched. The *maksa* dig the grave, and four of them carry the corpse to the clan burial ground and bury it. Everything at the funeral is in the hands of the *maksa*: lineal relatives of the deceased take no part.

It is thus evident that in practically every event and institution of both individual and social importance the *maksa*—the actual wife-takers—are not only ritually important but are indispensable. A Purum cannot be socially born, or be married, he cannot make a new house, or assume an office, or approach the gods, he cannot even die, without the aid of his wife-takers.

Let us now look at material prestations and at the extent of their significance. Rice beer and pig-meat are movable economic valuables which are highly prized by the Purum and appear in a variety of contexts. The common character of these contexts, the apparent significance of the transfer of these articles, leads to the inference that we have here symbolic usages which are characteristic of this type of society.

Beer is typically given as an offering to gods and ancestral spirits: viz., at the invocation of a certain deity on entering a new house, the assumption of office by a village official, the ceremony devoted to the deity of the gates, and the invocation of the ancestral spirits at the hair-cutting ceremony. Pigs are sacrificed to gods and ancestral spirits: viz., to secure release from diseases which particular deities are believed to cause, at the election of the village headman, at the worship of the deity of the gates, at the harvest "thank-offering," to the ancestral spirits at the hair-cutting ceremony, and at the invocation of the forest deity. Whatever else may be symbolized, it is clear that in these cases beer and pigs are prestations from inferiors to superiors.

With the general character of these items established, we may look at the social relationships in which they also figure. Pigs and rice beer are always given by village officials when they are elected to office; fixed numbers and quantities are given for a village feast by the elected person according to the grade of the position. When a man is honored with a certain feast, he gives three pigs and twenty pots of beer. The set numbers and quantities indicate some symbolic element, but there is no certain evidence in the literature of what the significance may be. But other situations are quite clear. When a man enters his novitiate to become a "medicine-man" he presents his prospective teacher with beer and asks formally for instruction; and when he becomes a master he makes a formal presentation to his teacher of a number of prescribed articles, first among which is rice beer. He shows "respect" to his teacher, and on the latter's death he presents rice beer to his household. Here there is certainly the expression of deference, a prestation from an inferior to a superior.

Fines are the only forms of punishment for delicts and are always levied in beer and pigs. There are other forms of valuables, including cash, with which compensation could be made and economic deprivation inflicted, but beer and pigs are the only permitted forms. In economic terms, the rice with which the beer is made would be an almost equally punitive fine, but it is the beer that has to be given. It is not completely explanatory that pigs and rice are prominent economic valuables in an agricultural society of this sort: the invariant form of the fine and the ban on economic equivalents point to a symbolic significance, which is evidently that of expressing submission, the recognition of inferior status, by a symbolic prestation to a superior.

This leads us to what is structurally the most important context, the relationship between affines. A man wishing to marry his son to a certain girl takes a present of rice beer to the girl's father, begging him not to be "angry," and if the latter agrees to the proposal he drinks it. Here there is a double significance: that of the character of the present; and the fact that it is the wife-taker who pays the visit, humbly acknowledges his inferiority, and makes the proposal which the other may refuse. We know already that at the wedding rice beer is taken from the groom's father and given to the wife's father, together with a pig-meat curry.

Wife-takers, then, give rice beer and pig-meat to their wife-givers, just as do mortals to the gods. There is no indication anywhere in the literature that the reverse might be possible. We have already seen that wife-takers are inferior to wife-givers, and in this transfer of symbolic goods we see this status difference expressed.

We have also seen that, structurally speaking, there is a cycle of women, these supreme "movable valuables" being communicated in one "direction." Opposed to this cycle there is now a cycle of rice beer and pigs going in the opposite direction. That is, there is a division of economic goods (or those which are accorded symbolic significance) into "masculine" and "feminine" goods in contrary cycles. In matrilateral alliance the masculine goods circulate in the opposite direction to that of the women, and feminine goods in the same direction as the women. If we take the rice beer and meat to be masculine goods, what are the Purum equivalents of feminine goods other than the women themselves? There is unfortunately little evidence about gift exchange, but the important fact is clearly stated that when a woman is sent to her husband's house she takes with her one or more of the following articles: cloth, a brass plate, a carrying-basket, a storage-basket for valuables, a chopper, a brass cup, and a loom. If we may assume that the chopper is a domestic utensil proper to a woman's use (the monograph tells us that women use choppers in clearing land, and that it is they who collect firewood), it is satisfyingly clear that all these articles can be regarded as feminine goods and appropriate to the feminine cycle of prestations. Most significantly, we must note the presence of two items—cloth and the loom—which in better-known Indonesian systems of matrilateral alliance are pre-eminently feminine goods.

This division into two classes of goods is not merely a rational extension of the sexual division of labor, for Purum women cultivate and harvest the rice, raise pigs, and manufacture both cloth and beer, i.e., goods which belong to both classes. The goods and their cycles are conventionally opposed in a symbolism which is far wider and more significant, ritually and socially, than the particularities of any one institution or field of activity.

We may now return to the interpretation of the role of the *maksa*. We have seen that there are highly important chains of unilateral transfers of women and goods, which we have called cycles. In one direction there is structurally a circulation of women and certain associated goods in a "feminine cycle," and in the opposite direction there is a circulation of certain other goods in a "masculine cycle." But the importance of the valuables in the masculine cycle must seem rather trivial when compared with the value of women. In fact, however, this cycle includes other values, so that there is more of a "balance" than at first appears. Purum bride-service lasts three years, and we may picture as part of the masculine cycle three-year "units" of masculine labor circulating as prestations in exactly the same way as the more tangible masculine goods. Not only this, but there is a more vital type of prestation—the indispensable ritual services rendered by wife-takers to wife-givers. We may perhaps see, then, in these opposed cycles and classes a balance between two sorts of values, each vital to the total society. If the wife-takers depend on their wife-givers for women and the continuance of their lines, so in a similar fashion wife-givers depend utterly on their wife-takers (*maksa*) for indispensable aid in all the major events of life.

Thus the system is not characterized by the one cycle of the initial model, consisting of a unidirectional circulation of women, important though this is, but by a reciprocal opposition of two cycles, masculine and feminine. There may seem a contradiction in the fact that the superior wife-givers transmit feminine goods, while the inferior wife-takers transmit masculine goods, but I am sure there is not. Wife-takers in other such societies are characterized by the type of goods they receive, and it is they who are associated with the feminine cycle, not the group from which feminine goods issue. Generalizing, we may say that a prestation must be appropriate to the character and status of the receiver, and that a group is associated with those goods which are given to it. Masculine goods are therefore proper to wife-givers, and feminine goods to wife-takers: wife-givers are associated in this way with the (superior) masculine cycle, and wife-takers with the (inferior) feminine cycle.

But this opposition is itself part of a dualistic system of symbolic classification in which pairs of opposite but complementary terms are analogically related as in the scheme in Table 9. To begin with, the oppositions are listed seriatim as they have been elicited in the exposition of the relevant facts; but I have added a number of others which I have not demonstrated. Since I have shown the principles and the pervasive nature of the classification in the major institutions of Purum society, it does not seem necessary to continue the demonstration in this place down to the last particular.

We see here, as elsewhere with prescriptive alliance, a mode of classification by which things, individuals, groups, qualities, values, spatial notions, and other ideas of the most disparate kinds are identically ordered within one system of relations. In particular, I would draw attention to the remarkable concordance and interconnection of social and symbolic structure. In spite of the fact that structurally there must be three cyclically related

95

lines in the alliance system, the basic scheme of Purum society is not triadic but dyadic. Any given alliance group is wife-taker and therefore inferior to another, but it is also wife-giver and therefore superior to another group in a different context. That is, alliance status is not absolute but relative. The distinction to

TABLE 9

SCHEME OF PURUM SYMBOLIC CLASSIFICATION

Left	Right
Ningan division	*Phumlil* division
Front	Back
Affines	Kin
Public	Private
Strangers	Family
Wife-takers (*tu, maksa*)	Wife-givers (*pu*)
Inferior	Superior
Female	Male
Below	Above
Inauspicious	Auspicious
Feminine goods	Masculine goods
women	pigs, buffaloes
cloth	rice beer
loom	ritual services
domestic articles	labor (bride-service)
Mortals	Gods, ancestral spirits
Sun	Moon
Earth	Sky
(North)	South
West	East
Bad death	Good death
Even	Odd
Death	Life
Profane	Sacred
Sexual activity	Sexual abstinence
Forest	Village
Famine	Prosperity
Evil spirits, ghosts	Beneficent spirits

be appreciated is that between the triadic *system* and its component dyadic *relation*. It is through this mode of relation that the social order concords with the symbolic order.

But in fact, though one may use these distinctive designations for convenience of description and analysis, what one is really dealing with in such a society as this is a classification, a system of categories, which orders both social life and the cosmos. That is, Purum social organization is ideologically part of a cosmological conceptual order and is governed identically by its ruling ideas.

Here, then, we have a structurally typical example of a society prescribing marriage with the "mother's brother's daughter." I would stress, though, that (considerations of ethnographic comprehensiveness aside) it does not exhibit all the kinds of complexity which may be associated with matrilateral alliance. For example, Purum society has no rigid social stratification, and accordingly its descent groups are not ranked; it is not a territorially expansive or politically turbulent society, expressing and confirming political dominance and subjection through the categories of the alliance system; it has no further institutional complications such as moieties; and the population is very small. Yet, in spite of its institutional simplicity, I imagine it will be thought complex enough.

Matrilateral alliance can be regarded as a simple and effective way of creating and maintaining counter-fissive relationships in a segmentary society. We may find it most convenient therefore to characterize this form of society by its marriage prescription, and we have reason to do so since women are the prime movable valuables, and their transmission is in certain respects the most important type of prestation; but this must not distract us from other and contrary cycles of exchange, nor ultimately from the complementary dyadic mode of relation which is fundamental to Purum culture. As Hocart, with his characteristic insight, wrote in 1933 about dual organization, "The system then is not based on marriage, but marriage is regulated by the system."[8] The present system is defined by asymmetry, and the asymmetric rule of marriage is only one particularly prominent instance of this feature.

It is primarily on this point that Homans and Schneider come to grief, though an attentive and unbiased reading of Lévi-Strauss could have led them to see it: ". . . matrimonial exchange is only a particular case of those forms of multiple exchange which embrace material goods, rights, and persons; these exchanges themselves seem to be interchangeable."[9] It will be recalled that Homans and Schneider charge Lévi-Strauss with an excessively formal analysis, and assert that "the forces he exiled have returned

[8] Hocart, 1933, p. 258. Cf. Lévi-Strauss, 1949, pp. 129–30.

[9] Lévi-Strauss, 1949, pp. 145–46.

to undo him."[10] But in fact he devotes a whole chapter to the wide range of prestations involved, with the express object of showing that the exchange of women is only one aspect of a "total phenomenon" of exchange; and he specifically denies that he in any way thinks that the exchange or gift of women is the sole means of establishing alliances in simple societies.[11] Although he has to restrict his detailed analyses to the examination of descent systems and rules of marriage (and still ends up with an enormous book), this emphasis on the total character of exchange runs throughout his work and even forms its concluding pages, where he brilliantly relates the marriage systems to other forms of "communication." Homans and Schneider, on the other hand, work with a model which is quite inapt to the study of themes of this scope or societies of this type.

The topic of generality raises two possible objections which might be made, both to Lévi-Strauss's work and to the present analysis, though neither of them really has more than a certain initial plausibility. First, in exchange we are dealing with a universal of human behavior, and it might therefore be thought that an explanation in terms of it is open to the same charge as psychological explanations, viz., that what is completely general cannot account for variant particulars. But it is not just exchange in general that plays such an important part here: it is one particular mode of exchange, *échange généralisé,* conceived as cyclic; and it takes place between groups, and groups of a certain kind, viz., lineal descent groups. Moreover, the notion of "exchange" really does help us to understand this type of marriage rule and social system, as nothing in Homans and Schneider's argument does.

A crucial question, of course, is why marriage with the "father's sister's daughter" is forbidden. By Lévi-Strauss's interpretation, the answer is clear: because it would be quite contrary to the established rules for the communication of women, by which the system is characterized and by which the relative status of the component descent groups of the society is defined. When we pursue the application of this notion of exchange into the analysis of other institutions, as I have done in outline for Purum society,

[10] Homans and Schneider, 1955, p. 59. Cf. "The models may . . . get too simple, and what Lévi-Strauss discards will live to undo him" (Homans, 1955, p. 136).

[11] Lévi-Strauss, 1949, pp. 66–86, 599.

we see that it is not only the exchange of women and the relations between descent groups that is in question, but that one and the same mode of prestation governs economic and religious relationships as well. And not only this, but the relation common to all these social institutions also receives cosmological expression. In other words, marriage with the patrilateral cross-cousin would not be simply an isolated act of wrongdoing, having limited (punitive) consequences just for the two individuals by whom it was perpetrated; but it would constitute an onslaught on the entire complex of identically ordered relationships which are the society, and on the symbolic classification which is its ideological life.

All this we are able to see thanks ultimately to the astonishingly fertile notion of "exchange" as an analytical concept, fashioned for us by Mauss and developed in the field of marriage by Lévi-Strauss. It is true that this is only a mediating concept, and that it alone could not bring the analysis quite to the point of radical understanding that I think we have reached here; but it is an essential notion, and it has done for us what a truly scholarly insight should do—it has made things plain. Would Homans and Schneider be prepared to claim as much now for their own theory? Is all this really to be explained, as they say, by "the Oedipus Complex"?

The second possible objection may be more briefly disposed of. I have tried to demonstrate that the fundamental mode of relation by which this type of society is articulated and through which it is to be understood is that of complementary dualism, and I approached this conclusion by way of the typical differential evaluation of right and left. Now a dualistic categorization of phenomena, and the symbolic opposition of the sides, are so common in history and in societies which we know directly as to appear natural proclivities of the human mind.[12] I think indeed that they are. But is not this part of my analysis, in its turn, analogous therefore to those features of a psychological argument which invalidate the latter? Durkheim has the short answer to this, viz., that a psychological explanation allows everything that is social to escape.[13] But my ultimate recourse to epistemology does the reverse: it permits us to see an instance of matrilateral alliance,

[12] Hertz, 1909. Cf. Needham, 1960d.

[13] Durkheim, 1901, p. 131.

in all its institutional aspects, in terms of a relation of complete generality to that society. Moreover, this type of elucidation is, I think, feasible to this degree only in systems of prescriptive alliance, so that the very pragmatic effectiveness of the interpretation is itself a characteristic feature of the type of society in question. None of this is true of an explanation of social phenomena in terms of psychological universals, and certainly not of Homans and Schneider's particular argument.

It all comes down to the matter of understanding what we are trying to understand. I claim that structural analysis, of the sort inaugurated in this field by Lévi-Strauss and developed here in the analysis of a particular society, does give understanding. On the other hand, by thus laying bare the empirical features of matrilateral alliance, with which any theory has to cope, it has become perfectly clear that Homans and Schneider's psychological analysis is based upon a disablingly partial command of the facts. This must be due to a certain extent to the nature of their intellectual interests, and to the type of theory which they had tentatively framed and which they desired to prove; but whether or not these inferences are justified, it is apparent that they did not first comprehend that which they purported to explain. At any rate, it is undeniable that they have in no way adequately carried out their proclaimed intention to relate the rule of marriage to other institutions;[14] whereas I think the present analysis has done so, and in a completely general fashion.[15]

[14] Homans and Schneider, 1955, p. 20. (Above, p. 29.)

[15] This does not at all mean, however, that I think my analysis is finally correct, or that it is the only structural interpretation which might be made.

Chapter Five

> If one knows the effective forces that de-
> termine the adoption of one marriage rule
> rather than another, the question which one
> creates more organic solidarity becomes ir-
> relevant to explanation.—HOMANS[1]

CONCLUSIONS

*In this final chapter I examine the claim of Homans and Schnei-
der that their theory "will predict what societies will adopt what
form [of unilateral cross-cousin marriage], and Lévi-Strauss's
theory will not."[2]*

I

As far as the matrilateral prescription is concerned, Homans
and Schneider's argument is wrong, and it is quite implausible
that it should be any less wrong about a patrilateral prescription.
But is there really anything for it to be right or wrong about? In
my summary characterization of Homans and Schneider's "patrilateral" instances[3] I stated that not one of them is based on a
patrilateral prescription. I must now support this conclusion by
looking at these cases in rather more conclusive detail. In considering them, it should be kept in mind that a patrilateral prescriptive system may be expected to distinguish categorically between the patrilateral and the matrilateral cross-cousin, and that
marriage with the latter must be forbidden; but that even these
features are not necessarily in themselves signs of the certain existence of such a system.

The Kandyu of Cape York Peninsula in northern Australia are
said quite clearly to marry the father's sister's daughter and to
taboo the mother's brother's daughter.[4] They are divided into

[1] Homans, 1955, p. 137.

[2] Homans and Schneider, 1955, p. 59; authors' emphasis.

[3] Pp. 56–57 above.

[4] McConnel, 1939–40, pp. 72, 437.

named moieties, but have no bilineal section-system.[5] In a letter to Homans and Schneider, Radcliffe-Brown expressed "doubt that the Kandyu rule is really patrilateral: a man may marry the daughter of his father's younger, but not elder, sister, and the daughter of a classificatory, not true, mother's brother."[6] Homans and Schneider admit that they would have been pleased to drop the Kandyu from their list, on the basis of this report, as the case is contrary to their hypothesis: i.e., since the Kandyu are patrilineal they should prefer marriage with the matrilateral, not the patrilateral, cross-cousin. But they decided nevertheless to "respect the printed sources" and leave them in. I am not bound by their principles in this matter, however, and if this is a more exact rendering of the facts of the case I shall accept it. It seems very unlikely that such detailed evidence should be unreliable, and especially from such an authority; and it is moreover a situation similar to that reported from other tribes in the area. I conclude therefore that there is no certain ground for believing that the Kandyu actually prescribe marriage exclusively with the patrilateral cross-cousin.

The Sherente of central Brazil are divided into patrilineal exogamous moieties, each consisting of four clans.[7] They distinguish terminologically between mother's brother's daughter and father's sister's daughter, and "a man may marry his father's sister's daughter, but not his maternal uncle's." Yet there is reported "a tendency to marry close matrilineal kin so long as the prohibited degrees are avoided."[8] It is not possible to tell from the monograph what are the extensions within the affine-moiety of the two types of cross-cousin. It may be that the prohibition on the mother's brother's daughter applies to the mother's clan and prevents a man marrying a woman from the same clan as his father, thus obviating an exclusive reciprocal alliance between two clans at the expense of general affinal solidarity. This would

[5] Thomson, 1935, p. 463.

[6] Homans and Schneider, 1955, p. 48.

[7] Since part of my theme is concern for the exact comprehension of the facts, I think I must observe that Homans and Schneider at one point describe the Sherente as having seven clans and at another as having six (1955, p. 49), whereas in fact they have eight (Nimuendajú, 1942, pp. 17, 19, 23).

[8] Nimuendajú, 1942, pp. 25–26.

be consistent with the marked ingenuity of Sherente social structure, which constantly counters by one institution the possibility of permanent segmentation occasioned by another. This arrangement, however, given the relationship terms recorded by Nimuendajú, would be the maximum extension of the mother's brother's daughter prohibition: it removes one clan from the range of an individual's potential spouses, but it does not thereby prescribe marriage with the father's sister's daughter or set up a concordant system of relations between groups. In any case, the relationship terms are puzzling in some respects, and it is not evident how they are to be related to the social structure described; and more recent investigations among the Sherente have in fact given further reason to doubt their accuracy.[9]

The Haida of the northwest coast of America are divided into exogamous matrilineal moieties, each comprising about twenty clans. The "preferred marriage is with a *sq'an* [FZD] of the same generation, though not necessarily a first cousin." It appears that only a cousin in the father's clan is a *sq'an*. A man ordinarily marries a woman of this category, but if he is heir to a chieftainship he usually marries a daughter of the maternal uncle whom he is to succeed.[10] The situation is not described with the

[9] Maybury-Lewis, 1958.

[10] Murdock, 1934a, p. 364; 1934b, pp. 235, 250. Homans and Schneider decide to "eliminate chiefs and the like from consideration, as introducing a complicating variable, that of rank" (1955, p. 33); but chiefs are certainly part of Haida society, and their marriage with the mother's brother's daughter is equally a Haida marriage custom, and they may not be eliminated from the analysis any more than from the society in which they occupy such an integral and important position. In any case, though it would certainly make sociology easier if we eliminated inconvenient facts, it will be generally conceded that it is precisely our task to deal with "complicating variables." Furthermore, though I do not need to press the matter with regard to this society, these chiefly marriages might well be taken as evidence against Homans and Schneider's theory, in that they may be interpreted as showing that sentiment is subordinate, in this case, to rank and political power. If this is so, what other factors might not have to be considered before the relative importance of sentiment could be gauged? In other societies, too, the complicating variables may be quite different, requiring to be isolated afresh, and their influence assessed, in each separate case. With such considerations we see again that, whether the issue is prescription or preference, it is unwise to rely upon a single ethnographic source and to restrict examination of this limited evidence to a search for only two features.

desirable ethnographic detail, but it is certain from this information that there is no prohibition on marriage with a matrilateral cross-cousin such as would be necessary to make the "preference" for the patrilateral cross-cousin into a prescription.

The Ila of central Africa permit marriage with the father's sister's daughter and prohibit it with the mother's brother's daughter, but the situation amounts to no more than this. The same terms of address are used for both the matrilateral and the patrilateral cross-cousin, "but though I address my mother's brother's daughter as *mwinangu* ('my wife') and she addresses me as *mulami* ('my husband') it does not follow that commerce between us would be allowed. Of the four possible cousin-marriages, therefore, the Ba-Ila nowadays allow only one. I may marry my father's sister's daughter, but as, according to the rules of relationship, she is *mukwesu* ['my sister'] to me, I ought not to marry her."[11] Quite clearly there is no patrilateral prescription, and we may infer that formerly this was even more certainly the case.[12]

The matrilineal Tismulun of the New Hebrides may marry either the father's sister's daughter or the mother's brother's daughter's daughter. "Such marriages were by no means compulsory, but were approved as correct." One informant's verbatim account of the marriage rules describes how he looks first at the mother's brother's daughter's daughter, then at the father's sister's daughter, and makes his decision on the basis of which he happens to like. If neither, then preferably he marries a woman "from his father's place," the Tismulun being patrilocal. Marriage with the mother's brother's daughter "is, it seems, to be prohibited."[13] The ethnography is far from clear on even fundamental points (the term for mother's brother's daughter, for instance, is not reported at all), and these data are from random notes posthumously edited; but the conclusion must be that mar-

[11] Smith and Dale, 1920, I, 317–19. Homans and Schneider neglect to report that the father's sister's daughter "ought not" to be married, or to consider with what justification they speak of a patrilateral preference in this case.

[12] A factual gloss on the ethnography, incidentally, is that the Ila system may actually not be bilineal (cf. Homans and Schneider, 1955, p. 31). Gluckman says that they "probably recognise as important mother's matrilineal and father's matrilineal groups—not father's patrilineal" (1956).

[13] Deacon, 1929, pp. 483, 486–87.

riage is not prescribed exclusively with the patrilateral cross-cousin.[14]

The Tlingit are divided into exogamous matrilineal moieties, members of each of which regard each other as siblings. The ideal marriage links a man with his father's clan or lineage, and "preferably" he marries the "father's sister or her daughter." This type of marriage is called a "royal marriage," as it is considered especially appropriate to the aristocracy; and it is thus typically practiced, it would appear, only by a minority. The dual organization is stressed to the extent that the paternal aunt is "ideally" the mother's brother's wife. The latter may be married as a widow in order to succeed to her deceased husband's title. Also, "a young woman of rank may expect to marry her father's heir, that is her paternal uncle or her cross-cousin (father's sister's son)"; so it is even more plainly evident that there is no ban on marriage with the mother's brother's daughter and consequently no prescription to marry the patrilateral cross-cousin.[15]

Finally, in the Trobriands the woman most suited in native eyes to be married is the father's sister's daughter or her daughter. The instance of this kind of marriage selected by Malinowski as illustration is the marriage of a chief's son. However, "a boy and girl who are the children of two brothers . . . may marry if they like," i.e., the father's brother's daughter may also be married. Also, marriage to mother's brother's daughter "is not inces-

[14] Homans and Schneider remark, with regard to the Tismulun, that "one structural fact is especially worth citing," viz., that in a matrilineal-patrilateral society the mother's brother's daughter's daughter is father's sister's daughter to Ego's sister's son, his matrilineal heir (1955, p. 43); but they do not expatiate on what they take to be the precise significance of this fact for the question under discussion.

It should be stressed, however, with regard to the relation of Homans and Schneider's argument to Lévi-Strauss's theory, and the applicability of their analysis to prescriptive systems, that this is the case only in a system in which it is postulated that marriage with the patrilateral cross-cousin is prescribed ("regularly followed," as Homans and Schneider put it), not merely preferred. If Ego's MBS is not constrained to marry Ego's sister, and without exercising a patrilateral preference marries another category of woman, then Ego's MBDD will not be FZD to his ZS. This emphasizes again the need to distinguish prescription from preference, and illustrates Homans and Schneider's inconsistency of argument (cf. above, pp. 12, 16).

[15] De Laguna, 1952, pp. 2, 5–7.

tuous, but is viewed with disfavor and happens only rarely"—but it is evidently possible and is certainly not prohibited as it would have to be in a patrilateral prescriptive system.[16]

So we see that not one of Homans and Schneider's patrilateral instances really is prescriptive, even though I have employed only minimal arguments. I have not, that is, even had to make systematic analyses of the relationship terminologies (where they are available) or present other equally cogent proofs that none of these societies prescribes marriage with the patrilateral cross-cousin.

Not only this, but it seems that nowhere in the world is there such a society. When *Marriage, Authority, and Final Causes* was published, Eggan wrote in his review that "we have no examples of a fully functioning system [based on patrilateral cross-cousin marriage] comparable to that for matrilateral cross-cousin marriage";[17] and I also wrote at the same time that "there is no sure evidence that exclusive patrilateral cross-cousin marriage is practiced by any society at all."[18] I have since searched diligently in the ethnographic literature for such a case,[19] but without encountering anything of the sort or any evidence from which the probable existence of such a system could be inferred. Perhaps more significantly, in the intervening years since the publication of these reviews, Homans and Schneider have nowhere, to my knowledge, adduced a single example of a patrilateral prescriptive system. The reason, I think, is that neither they nor anyone else can: a patrilateral system of prescriptive alliance simply does not exist.

On purely empirical grounds, then, Homans and Schneider's theory is without application. They claim to be able to "predict" what societies will adopt what form of unilateral cross-cousin marriage, and to explain why one type of society "adopts" the matrilateral form and another the patrilateral. The argument, I repeat, is about prescriptions; but since there is no evidence for the existence of any society with a patrilateral prescription there is nothing to be predicted, no adoption to be explained. What-

[16] Malinowski, 1929, pp. 81, 86–87.

[17] Eggan, 1956, p. 403.

[18] Needham, 1956, p. 108.

[19] See Needham, 1958*b*, pp. 212–17, for the examination of further "patrilateral" cases not in Homans and Schneider's list.

ever the rule of descent, and wherever the locus of jural authority, no society has a patrilateral prescription. As far as the ethnographic evidence goes, there is only *one* form of prescriptive unilateral cross-cousin marriage, the matrilateral.

II

So much for the facts of the matter, the facts to which Homans and Schneider's argument is supposed to apply. My own argument could therefore end at this point. It could have ended at a number of previous points as well, of course, but this is the crowning objection so far encountered, and to most effects and purposes a final one.

It may however be thought that if one wrecks a theory one is under an obligation to erect another and better one in its place; and that I am not free, then, to terminate the argument at this point, without saying just why it is that patrilateral prescriptive alliance does not exist. Bluntly, I think this is nonsense, though it is an understandable enough reaction; and I mention it here only because it has been specifically brought to my attention as an issue to be reckoned with.[20] It is of course all very well to be able to propose immediately a better substitute for a hypothesis that has been refuted; but there is no ground whatever, certainly no methodological necessity, for insisting that this must always be done. I claim that Homans and Schneider's argument, in the respects defined, is decisively refuted; and I am perfectly at liberty, in all scholarly responsibility, to stop here.

Nevertheless, I shall proceed, for two reasons: (1) Lévi-Strauss himself writes in places as though a patrilateral prescription did exist, and Homans and Schneider could respond that in this respect at least their theory has applicability; (2) there is in fact an answer to why societies possess the matrilateral rule but not the patrilateral, and moreover one that is directly relevant to Lévi-Strauss's theoretical concern with solidarity.

[20] I should not, in normal circumstances, have thought this worth doing; and I do so here chiefly because, in response to certain observations in my 1958 Purum analysis, I was advised by one interested reader that I was under an obligation to "put up [i.e., a better theory] or shut up." I do not know how general such a view may be, but it appears that it needs to be taken into account.

To the extent that Lévi-Strauss speaks of a patrilateral system I have of course to argue not only that Homans and Schneider are mistaken but that he also is. What exactly, then, does he say? It is remarkable, in the first place, that only an extremely small proportion of his book deals with patrilateral alliance, and then for the most part in a formal manner and not with reference to empirical data. But he does say, after all, that marriage with the mother's brother's daughter is far more common than with the father's sister's daughter,[21] and furthermore he defines what he takes to be the diagnostic features of an actual patrilateral system.[22] At a few points, also, he adduces what he thinks are empirical examples of such a rule of marriage, and we ought to look at these first.

The Mara of Australia are one example, but not in a full sense: i.e., patrilateral marriage is only an alternative possibility, and even this is apparently regarded by Lévi-Strauss as merely a survival.[23] The Aluridja are cited as another example, but they are said to practice marriage with the father's sister's daughter only exceptionally, though Lévi-Strauss surmises that such marriage may formerly have been general among them.[24] The Munda system is merely thought to be best analyzable on the assumption that formerly it was based on marriage to father's sister's daughter.[25] The only society definitely claimed actually to practice exclusive patrilateral cross-cousin marriage are the Kandyu,[26] but Lévi-Strauss does not undertake an analysis of the evidence, which in any case is exiguous and, as we have just seen, almost surely misleading. So these examples really do little more than bring us back to the fact that Lévi-Strauss's argument concerning patrilateral alliance is almost entirely formal. He is not correct in thinking that empirical instances of such a system do exist, and certainly not as far as the cases he cites are concerned; but this fact does not at all deprive his argument of value, as we shall see.

Let us continue now with a formal analysis on the lines that Lévi-Strauss has laid down. He maintains, it will be recalled, that patrilateral marriage is not a system but a procedure, and that it

---

[21] Lévi-Strauss, 1949, pp. 528, 554.

[22] Pp. 254, 274–76.

[23] Pp. 248–52.

[24] Pp. 253–54.

[25] Pp. 529–31.

[26] Pp. 251, 545.

is incapable of securing a general organic solidarity. He does not remark, however, that a model of a patrilateral prescriptive system (as in Fig. 2) is capable of an integral interpretation. As Homans and Schneider[27] and van Wouden[28] have pointed out, within each genealogical level there is in fact a cycle of *échange généralisé,* just like the characteristic cycle of matrilateral alliance. The real difference between this system and a matrilateral system lies in the alternation of direction in which women are transferred between lines in succeeding generations; but as a formal representation of a hypothetical social system it surely appears to be an organically solidary arrangement. Homans and Schneider even suggest that, since specialization in marriage is determined in such a system by generation as well as by line, patrilateral marriage may even make for greater organic solidarity than matrilateral.[29] But how valid, simply in a formal sense, is this interpretation?

The central feature of any patrilateral system, however it may be conceived, is the alternation; and this is directly and ineluctably entailed by the exclusively patrilateral prescription. But is this prescription itself even possible? Is it feasible, that is, to determine a category of relationship whose genealogical specifications as cross-cousin shall be defined solely through the father? If we consider the minimal specifications, FZD and MBD, it certainly seems so; and on Homans and Schneider's premise of first-cousin marriage, which is all they take into account, it appears at first sight to be a practicable rule. But this is not the case.

In the study of systems of prescriptive alliance the arbitrary restriction to first cousins, as we have seen in the matrilateral case, mutilates irremediably the social facts which are to be understood, and precludes any possibility of explanation. We have to pose the problem in classificatory terms, defining the positions in question not minimally but by their more extended specifications. The MMBDD, for instance, is thus a cross-cousin, though of what status will depend on the particular system within which the specification is made. Now in our hypothetical patrilateral system (Fig. 2), the FZD is structurally MMBDD also: i.e., mar-

[27] Homans and Schneider, 1955, p. 13.

[28] Van Wouden, 1956, p. 206.

[29] Homans and Schneider, 1955, p. 13.

riage is prescribed with the category of person whose specifications are at once FZD and MMBDD. But in what sense is this category that of "patrilateral cross-cousin"? Is the mother's mother's brother's daughter's daughter really a *patrilateral* relative?

Let us glance at the specifications in question in different types of alliance system. In a matrilateral system, to begin with, the equation FZD = MMBDD cannot be made (Fig. 1). In this system, not only is FZD distinct from MBD, but the MBD is herself equivalent to MMBDD: i.e., MMBDD is opposed to FZD as matrilateral to patrilateral cross-cousin. Next, in a classical two-section system (Fig. 6) FZD = MBD = MMBDD: i.e., the prescribed spouse is the bilateral cross-cousin, and this is what the

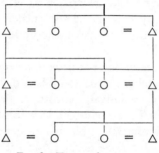

Fig. 6.—Two-section system

MMBDD is in this system—a bilateral relative. Precisely the same is the situation in a four-section system. We could examine other systems, but these simple and typical instances are ample for the present purpose. It may further be observed, though, that the equations and distinctions under examination are the same in all of these (except the four-section system, which is bilineal) whether descent is patrilineal or matrilineal. In all of them the MMBDD is, in one aspect of her status at least, a matrilateral relative; and in the section-systems she is a bilateral relative. Now this is the case in our hypothetical patrilateral system as well. As MMBDD, the prescribed category of spouse is a *matrilateral* relative; and in her fuller definition as FZD/MMBDD she is a *bilateral* relative.

In terms of laterality of prescription, therefore, there are in this respect not three but only two kinds of cross-cousin with whom marriage can possibly be prescribed: the matrilateral and (in one or other definition of the status) the bilateral.

In a matrilateral system, patrilateral and matrilateral cross-cousins are structurally quite distinct, and the very viability of the system depends utterly on the maintenance of this absolute distinction. In the hypothetical patrilateral system, on the other hand, whatever genealogical exclusions (e.g., MBD) are made by the rule of marriage, the prescribed cross-cousin is necessarily a bilateral relative; and it is impossible to determine an alliance category whose genealogical specifications as cross-cousin shall be exclusively patrilateral. Whatever the supposed solidary consequences of such a system, therefore, it is not in fact based on prescribed patrilateral cross-cousin marriage.

III

I could of course be mistaken in this formal argument, but it does not in any case exhaust the possibilities of objection to the proposed patrilateral system. There are grave pragmatic considerations to be taken into account as well, and these would in themselves be refutation enough, even without argument of a formal kind. What we have to look at now is whether this model could adequately represent a society in terms of the social life of people on the ground.

In this scheme, a lineal descent group must be clearly divided into generations of marriageable men and women, and each descent group must be similarly and congruently divided in order to make the alternating exchange-relationship possible. Only thus is it conceivable that each group should function as a group alternately as wife-givers to another group and as wife-takers from that group. It is barely conceivable that such a system could work with the aid of a conventional division into arbitrary genealogical levels, and that the rule of marriage should be ceremonially declared at intervals (cf. an age-set system), so that one generation so defined would marry in one direction (in terms of the diagram) and the succeeding generation in the reverse direction. This might be feasible in a small-scale society with optimum communications, but it is an arrangement so at the mercy of a multitude of factors that it would be unlikely to constitute a viable form of marriage regulation. Moreover, whatever its practical features, it is unsatisfactory as a theoretical answer, since the conventional generations would not be defined by any feature of the alliance system itself, but merely by an institution contingent to it.

The only invariably effective means of establishing such an alternation of affinal role by generations as the model demands is by some kind of bilineal section-system, in which a man and his son would necessarily belong to different sections. But a three-section system (to accord with the three lines) is impossible, and a system based on a multiple of three would not serve; and in any case a bilineal section-system would by definition exclude the possibility of an exclusively unilateral prescription.

In short, it does not appear that there is any way of securing the clear and congruent division of all participant descent groups into conventional generations which is essential to the system. If there is, Homans and Schneider have not told us what it is—and indeed it is apparent that they have not realized that there is any difficulty involved.

This is only the first, and most obvious, of the practical difficulties in trying to order people's social lives by this scheme. Most of the others are really subsumed under the other major objection, viz., that in accordance with the typical features of lineal descent systems in general, and prescriptive alliance systems in particular, a descent group must be assumed to act *as a corporate group* in occupying alternately the status of wife-givers and of wife-takers. But consider what the consequences of this feature would be for such a society as the Purum. It is not only women, remember, whose communication or exchange is effected by the system, but a whole complex of prestations in which women are just one item; and it has to be supposed that in a patrilateral system—i.e., a system of prescriptive alliance parallel in all typical respects to the matrilateral, save for the different prescription— this entire scheme of prestations would have to be reversed in each succeeding conventional generation.

Take any two local alliance groups. In the first generation, A will be wife-givers to B, who are in the inferior position of wife-takers; A will give all the items of the "feminine" class of goods to B, and will receive in turn only goods of the "masculine" class, including the extraordinary variety of ritual services affecting every event of either individual or group importance. This is all quite clear, and exhibits the same complete distinction of complementary statuses as in the matrilateral system. But for the members of the next generation all this is reversed. For members of A, group B—which is inferior to members of the senior generation of their group—will now be superior, and all the goods and services which B owes to A in the first generation will now be owed by members of A to members of B in this second generation. This is confusing, as well as difficult to effect; but once the respective statuses are redefined, the scheme of prestations can be maintained within this second generation just as well as in the first. All right, but then at the next generation again everything is reversed once more; and so on.

This is a strange enough situation in general terms, but now consider further what happens when two such groups meet as groups, at an event such as the contraction of marriage in which members of two groups and of at least two successive generations

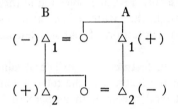

Fig. 7.—Affinal status in a patrilateral system

participate at the same time. It is easy to stipulate in a matrilateral system that B, as wife-takers, will acknowledge their inferior status by going to A with masculine presents which express their inferiority, for this is a continuing status occupied by successive generations for as long as the relationship between the two groups lasts. But whatever will happen where this status alternates by generation? Senior members will stand in the relation of $A > B$, while the next junior generation will be in that of $A < B$ (Fig. 7). If A_1 acts on behalf of his son, A_2, he will be putting himself in a position of inferiority to B_1, his own wife-taker, to whom he himself is superior within his own generation; and B_1, acting as custodian of his daughter, will be in the position of wife-giver to the son of A_1, his own wife-giver. In one status, B_1 should go to his superior, A_1, with masculine goods; in another, B_1 should himself assert superiority by receiving A_1 and accepting such goods from him. And, once again, let me stress that the relations between these structural positions involve not only the cession of women, but all the items of the system of prestations which comprise the economic and ritual intercourse between the units of the society. This, it will be agreed, is a picture of sheer confusion.

It could be protested that these differential statuses are not necessary concomitants of the proposed system, and of course this is true. But in constructing a hypothetical system we do best normally to endow it with the attributes of known systems which are structurally cognate; and in this case we have adopted typical features of the only known type of unilateral prescriptive alliance system, surely a reasonable procedure. Moreover, if the protest were admitted, we should be dealing with a lineal descent system in which affinal status was undifferentiated, a situation as empirically unexpected as the system is strange. That is, this feature would itself constitute a further objection to the proposed system. In any case, though, this matter of affinal status is only a partial and introductory expression of the self-destructive character of the system.

With the known features of matrilateral alliance in mind, let us look again at the features of the total system supposedly created by a patrilateral system with its perpetual alternation. The situation proves to be such as is found in no lineal descent system anywhere. It is not simply that individual affines are involved in contradictory relationships, but that the descent groups are similarly and more seriously affected. It will be remembered that I characterized matrilateral alliance as having the effect of countering fissive tendencies in a segmentary society. The kind of fission in question is a familiar theme in the study of lineal descent systems, e.g., in analyzing the solidary effects of age-set systems or ceremonial or religious institutions which bring otherwise independent groups into relation with each other. The fissive tendency envisaged is always lineal, something natural enough in a lineal descent system.

But look at what we have in our hypothetical patrilateral system: not merely lineal fission, but *lateral* as well, by generations, and not simply a disruptive tendency which may be checked by particular institutions, but an accomplished structural feature which is the defining and inescapable consequence of the rule on which the system is founded. The coherent working of the system of prestations which largely comprises the life of the society is in fact rigidly confined within only one generation at a time. This means that the descent group cannot be a corporate group: its solidarity is destroyed by reason of the fact that successive generations within it are separated by their opposed interests and statuses. The characters by which a lineal descent group exhibits its corporative nature unite in this case only members of alternate generations; and its unity in relation to other groups is also destroyed by the alternation of status which prevents its members concerting as a corporate group, bound together by common status and interests, in opposition to other such unitary groups.

A prescriptive alliance system is constituted by the factors of descent and alliance, the one complementary to the other in assuring and perpetuating social order. But in a patrilateral system descent is disintegrated by alliance.

What I claim, then, is that a hypothetical patrilateral system would be so obviously difficult to work as to be reckoned for practical purposes socially impossible.[30] In other words, as a solidary arrangement it would be, to say the least, less effective than a matrilateral system—which is precisely Lévi-Strauss's essential point. Admittedly, the argument by which we have arrived at this conclusion is not Lévi-Strauss's, but the result comes directly from taking his idea seriously, whereas Homans and Schneider neglect utterly to do so.[31]

By their disregard of this factor it might even be inferred that they think the issue of differential solidarity, in comparing the matrilateral and patrilateral systems, to be inherently fallacious. This would be an extremely difficult position to maintain, for it would amount to denying that some social arrangements work more efficiently, with fewer inconsistencies, than others. But we have, on the contrary, ample examples of arrangements which are rare or unknown precisely on these grounds: e.g., certain configurations of attitudes between close relatives whose conse-

[30] On this point in particular I should like to emphasize that the argument is far from exhaustive. There are a number of other cogent criticisms by which this same conclusion can be arrived at, but it is neither necessary nor appropriate to work them all out here.

[31] Cf. "The authors did not take seriously Lévi-Strauss's statement: 'marriage with father's sister's daughter is not capable of attaining any other form than a multitude of little closed systems . . .'" (Eggan, 1956, pp. 402–3).

quences would be so disruptive as to make them perhaps impossible;[32] systems of parallel descent;[33] matrilateral alliance with an Omaha terminology exactly equating mother and mother's brother's daughter. These examples are not adduced teleologically, in the sense that people are held to recognize that certain institutions are socially useful or convenient, and to strive purposefully to attain them. They may or may not do so, depending on the society and on the institutions in question. But there is little reason to think that they have difficulty in recognizing, or compunction in abandoning, institutions which are unwieldy without offering acknowledged compensatory advantages. Of course, they would have to abandon one arrangement in favor of another which they will normally have conceived beforehand, and to this extent there may be a purposive element; but this is a far cry from the situation, imagined by Homans and Schneider and foisted upon Lévi-Strauss, of members of a society cogitating on the attainment of "organic solidarity" and striving to achieve an ultimate arrangement satisfying this abstract sociological criterion.[34]

As a matter of fact, though, there are two points in Homans and Schneider's own book where they themselves adduce such considerations. At one, they consider the logically possible class of patrilineal-matrilocal societies, and they cogently conclude that its "structural difficulties and instabilities go far to explain why societies of [this] class do not seem to exist."[35] At the other, they concede that there is at least one situation in which matrilateral cross-cousin marriage is clearly "better" than patrilateral, viz., where lineages are ranked as among the Kachin. "If the lineages of a society differ in social rank, and one of the aspects of the relationship between a superior lineage and a subordinate one is that the former gives women to the latter (or vice versa), then mother's brother's daughter marriage is practicable as a formal

[32] Lévi-Strauss, 1958, p. 83.

[33] Maybury-Lewis, 1960.

[34] See p. 23 above. It may further be emphasized that in fact Lévi-Strauss elaborates on the possibility of an extreme multiplicity of origin of certain marriage rules, precisely in order to contrast the generality of a structural interpretation which is free of such contingent developments as this collective decision (1949, pp. 156–60).

[35] Homans and Schneider, 1955, pp. 54–55; cf. Leach, 1951, p. 25.

structure and father's sister's daughter marriage is not. The latter would destroy the ranking by making any one lineage alternately superior and subordinate to another."[36] The second example is especially telling, since it is so analogous to the patrilateral situation I have just been examining. An essential systematic difference, of course, is that in the Kachin situation the status difference is that of absolute social rank, whereas in the latter it is that of relative affinal status; but this difference is analytically immaterial when we examine the continuing relationship between any two lines. Now if Homans and Schneider can admit this kind of solidarity-argument in these cases, why do they refuse to do so in considering Lévi-Strauss's analysis of the patrilateral system? Only, I think, because they mistake Lévi-Strauss's argument in the ways I have indicated. They misread him as maintaining that a rule of marriage is consciously adopted with the purpose of securing an ultimate "organic solidarity," whereas what he is saying is that one system prevails because it works better than another—which is exactly the kind of argument which they themselves correctly employ in these two instances.

To proceed, then, with the pragmatic objections to the proposed patrilateral system, there is still another important point to be made. The hypothetical patrilateral system I have been dealing with, as represented in Figure 2, is patrilineal. But according to Homans and Schneider a patrilateral system should on the contrary be matrilineal. Now if such a system could exist, and if their theory were right, consider the factor of marital residence. A matrilineal-patrilocal system would probably not be viable, and the least to be said about a patrilocal rule of residence is that it would entail serious difficulties as a working arrangement. A matrilocal rule, on the other hand, would entail the kinds of disruptive tension which we have seen among the Belu. Whatever the rule of residence, therefore, Homans and Schneider's premise that a patrilateral system will be matrilineal means that it is even less likely to be a solidary arrangement.

Finally, even if all these arguments were invalid, and a patrilateral system were feasible, what would be the point of it? To the limited extent, and in the limited contexts, that it possesses the social advantages of simplicity, regularity, and freedom from contradictory statuses, these are all such as are secured in an in-

[36] Homans and Schneider, 1955, pp. 13-14.

comparably more satisfactory form by matrilateral alliance. All the disadvantages, on the other hand, stem solely from the patrilateral prescription. Why then should any society ever order itself in this way? It may well be that any logically or socially possible arrangement, however contrived or however aberrant from the usual forms of social life, will be found in some society somewhere and for some time; and it is certainly conceivable, simply on this ground, that members of a certain society may have given the patrilateral prescription a trial. But even if they had, and if—contrary to all theoretical expectation—it had worked, what possible reason would they have had to keep it? Structurally, a matrilateral prescriptive alliance system is beautifully simple, stable, and adaptive. A patrilateral system is a paradigm of instability and confusion.

My argument, then, is that a prescriptive alliance system based on exclusive patrilateral cross-cousin marriage not only does not exist, but on both formal and pragmatic grounds cannot exist—and *this* is the answer to the problem of unilateral "choice."

IV

The argument has centered on the issue of solidarity, of systematic viability, raised by Lévi-Strauss, and it is a structural, not a psychological, argument. A methodological point that it makes is that one can have little idea what the consequences of a patrilateral prescription might be unless one first knows what the features of the matrilateral system actually are; and in this respect also Homans and Schneider's failure to acquaint themselves with the facts has again nullified their argument.

So far I have been arguing about the particularities of unilateral cross-cousin marriage, and in these respects I rest my case. But before I end, there are certain more general theoretical considerations that I should touch upon. Their focus is the validity of the notion of "cause" in sociological analysis, and especially as employed by Homans and Schneider. Cause is the central and continuing theme of their monograph, but the question is never raised whether it is a valid or useful procedure to seek "the cause" of an institution.

To begin with, the kind of cause they are interested in is psychological: "In the locus of authority and the personal, sentimental interests it precipitates we have provided an *efficient-cause* type of explanation."[37] They do not ask, reasonably, what ultimately causes the particular allocation of authority; but, given a certain locus of jural authority, they say that it is *sentiment* which is the cause of the associated rule of marriage. Patripotestal authority, for example, causes certain opposed sentiments such that the relationship with the mother's side will be close and affectionate, and this sentimental relationship is the cause of matrilateral cross-cousin marriage. Could anything be simpler? Very well, but when we consider the most successful explanations of social behavior could not this very simplicity be taken as an indication that the explanation given here is unlikely to be right? I do not think there is one convincing explanation of this type in all anthropological literature.

An admirably conducted and conclusive demonstration of the invalidity of a psychological causal explanation of this kind is Leach's brilliant analysis of Malinowski's argument concerning, among other things, the alleged preference for marriage to father's sister's daughter among the Trobrianders. This case is peculiarly apt to the present discussion, since Homans and Schneider cite the Trobrianders as a matrilineal-patrilateral instance and claim that the evidence is all in accordance with their theory: ". . . we were right for the right reasons."[38]

Malinowski's argument, it will be recalled, is that marriage to father's sister's daughter is "a compromise between father-love and matriliny"[39] which permits a man to circumvent the rule of matrilineal inheritance in favor of his own son (Fig. 8). The rightful heir of Ego (1) is his sister's son (2), but he does not like to transmit valuable rights to his heir to the detriment of his own son (3); so during his lifetime he gives his son whatever he can safely alienate from the heir. These gifts provoke the latter's resentment, and may lead to dissension between him and the son. But if the son marries his father's sister's daughter (4) a compromise can be reached. The taboo which prevents a man knowing anything about the sexual affairs of his sister prevents him objecting to the marriage; and in any case it may

[37] P. 59; authors' italics.

[38] P. 44.

[39] Malinowski, 1929, p. 81.

be contracted while he is too small to understand how it affects him. The son in this case lives in his father's village, instead of following the usual matrilocal rule, and enjoys the property there during his father's lifetime. Moreover, he now has claims on the heir, as his wife's brother, who has to make him gifts of food and is conventionally bound to be his friend and ally. And even though the heir will still come into his rightful inheritance, a compromise will continue to be wrought in the next generation. He in his turn has to transmit the rights to his own sister's son (5)—who is the son's son of the first man. That is, there is an indirect patrilineal inheritance within a strictly matrilineal sys-

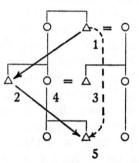

Fig. 8.—Patrilateral marriage and matrilineal inheritance

tem. Note that this is a psychological argument precisely analogous to that of Homans and Schneider: the sentiment of father for son, of the kind posited by them in a matrilineal system of this sort, is the efficient cause of the preference for patrilateral cross-cousin marriage.

But Leach has demonstrated that the argument is unsatisfactory. Actual occurrences of patrilateral cross-cousin marriage in the Trobriands seem to be rare, and to be confined to the families of chiefs; and even in these cases Malinowski has not shown that the Trobrianders themselves think of this form of marriage as a "tortuous legal subterfuge" of the kind outlined above. Also, when marriage with the patrilateral cross-cousin does occur, residence is abnormal: the husband, instead of taking his wife to his own hamlet, goes on living in his father's village. But such behavior is altogether exceptional, and the only example that Malinowski cites is that of a chief's son. Now since chiefs receive their "tribute" in the form of certain gifts of food (*urigubu*) from their wives' brothers, it is a matter of political importance who receives the *urigubu* payments of the chief himself. Leach then persuasively argues that, for the aristocratic Trobrianders to whom Malinowski's main evidence relates, it is actually bilateral cross-cousin marriage that is practiced, thus permitting chiefly groups to exchange *urigubu* without prejudice to the political status of either. Finally, the principle involved in patrilateral cross-cousin marriage is explained thus: "Whoever marries the sister of the chief's heir is potentially in a structurally superior position, for the chief's heir must pay him tribute. By marrying this girl to his own son, and then insisting that the son stays where he is, the chief is not 'favoring his son,' he is protecting the rights of his heir. The son pays *urigubu* to his father the chief. . . . The preferred marriage with a father's sister's daughter, in so far as it exists, has nothing to do with the affection of fathers for sons. It is simply a straightforward mechanism in the working of the political structure."[40]

These summary accounts are indeed summary, and Leach's argument in particular cannot really be appreciated outside the context of the far wider analysis that he makes; but the example is a good one, and though I cannot reproduce it in proper detail it does make my points. These are: (1) that a unicausal argument to explain the form of marriage is quite ineffective; (2) that a highly general sentiment is irrelevant to the sociological explanation of the alleged preference; and (3) that a correct understanding is to be obtained not by simple psychological inferences but by intensive structural analysis of complexes of facts of the most disparate institutional kinds.

It should be noted, moreover, that the import of this example is not contingent on the correctness of Leach's argument. Even if it were wrong it would still make my case; for it is a vastly more sophisticated and convincing analysis than Malinowski's, and although it might be proved inexact in some respects, any argument intended to improve upon it would have to be of the same type.

[40] Leach, 1958*a*, pp. 138–39. Homans and Schneider's reference to Trobriand marriage is incidentally singled out as an example of "unjustified theoretical speculation."

V

It seems to be fairly certain that causal arguments in terms of sentiments (or any other psychological factors) have not been of pragmatic value in sociological analysis. But it is not only psychological causes which are at issue. The question is whether causal arguments as such are of explanatory value in the analysis of social institutions.

This of course is an enormous topic, and I shall not attempt to develop it here. I merely make certain general and acknowledged observations. The first is that causal analysis is only one method of understanding: it is not a paradigm of all explanation to which sociological analysis must conform. Whether we are encouraged to employ it depends on its pragmatic success; but even in physics, the most spectacularly successful sphere of human understanding, the notions of cause and causal chain have proved to be devoid of theoretical value.[41] Whatever the extent of the analogy between the exact sciences and the so-called social sciences, it is surely disquieting that this should be the case precisely in the field where these notions might be expected to be of most applicability. I do not see how it could be pretended, on whatever grounds, that they are likely to be of any more use in social anthropology. Second, the idea of a single efficient cause does not appear to have been fruitful, or even thought likely to be so, in any discipline at all. In Homans and Schneider's argument it is a single factor—the locus of jural authority—which is the determinant of so much else; and even within their comprehension of the facts, it is difficult to see how they could have thought any single feature to be so systematically consequential, either in marriage or in any other sphere of social life. I do not wish to argue these points, but merely adduce them in order to suggest that on the most general methodological grounds one immediately has reason, when confronted with a theory such as Homans and Schneider's, to suspect it of being radically misconceived. My own argument in this book is, I think, one more demonstration of the principle that any causal, and particularly unicausal, explanation in comparative sociological analysis is unlikely to be right.

Part of this issue, but distinct enough to deserve separate com-

[41] Waissmann, 1959; Toulmin, 1953, pp. 119–25.

ment, is Homans and Schneider's use of the words "determine" and "predict." What does it mean, for example, to say that authority is an important "determinant" of social behavior?[42] It implies literally that there is a primal situation characterized solely by a certain allocation of authority, and that subsequently other features of social behavior appear whose form is caused by this factor. But this is untestable in relation to the evidence we have been examining. What we are given factually is certain types of social organization, defined partly by locus of authority and allegedly manifesting correlated modes of behavior. Authority may be functionally related to these modes, and may even be an analytical feature of first importance, but it cannot be asserted that it determines them. The statement is significant only on the assumption that societies practicing unilateral cross-cousin marriage have developed from lineal descent systems with certain allocations of authority but without such marriage. This, however, is a historical or evolutionary proposition which cannot be proved for the societies in question. It appears plausible, but that is another matter; and anyway other propositions could also be plausibly advanced.

As for prediction, Homans and Schneider frame both their special hypothesis and their general theory in the future tense (societies with certain marriage rules "will be" those with certain characteristics, the form of marriage "will be determined by" certain factors), and they explicitly claim to be able to "predict" what societies will adopt what form of marriage. This all sounds very scientific, but what does it really amount to?

The obvious first consideration is that "prediction" applies to events: things are in a certain state at t_1 and it is predicted (foretold, prophesied, announced beforehand) that at t_2 they will be in a certain other state. In this light, how are Homans and Schneider's "predictions" to be interpreted? Clearly, the future tense in their propositions is purely figurative: in both of them the present tense could as well (indeed, more validly) be employed, and they would then be seen for what they really are, viz., simple statements of association. They have in fact no genuine predictive value: they merely assert an established empirical association, such that if Homans and Schneider are told that a society is, for example, patrilineal, patripotestal, and practices

[42] Homans and Schneider, 1955, p. 58.

unilateral cross-cousin marriage, they will then feel confident in inferring that the rule of marriage is matrilateral. But to infer from a partial description of a complex phenomenon that other features will also, on further investigation or the revelation of additional information, be found to co-exist, is not prediction in any scientific or useful sense. What we have to assume, to test Homans and Schneider's ability to predict, is that they are given an ample description—answering all the questions which they think relevant to the issue—of a lineal descent system at t_1 and that this society then adopts at t_2 a rule of unilateral cross-cousin marriage. Only then should we have a truly predictive situation. But they do not claim to be able to cope with such a situation,[43] and in fact it is scarcely attainable. Nor do they cite historical evidence relating to societies actually practicing prescriptive alliance such as would support the postulated developmental process and confirm the predictive capability of their propositions. Further, there are certain features of these systems which (as I shall show elsewhere) entail their marked and rapid disintegration in the conditions under which we have come to learn of them. So any possible predictions are likely in any case to be about changes from prescriptive alliance into systems of different kinds, not at all the kind of prediction for which Homans and Schneider's propositions appear literally to be designed.

In sum, on both logical and factual grounds their propositions are operationally inconsequential. That is, they are empirical generalizations, not abstract formulas capable of theoretical manipulation or novel application. As such, however their terms may be defined or their application directed, they are fallacious, they are devoid of predictive value, and they cannot isolate any causes of the marriage rules in question.

VI

Is Homans and Schneider's theory then sociologically quite misdirected? I should not claim as much. It might be worth further examination as far as preferences alone are concerned, though the restriction of its scope to first cousins would have

[43] P. 59.

to be abandoned. I think it most unlikely, even then, that the psychological processes they posit could survive the criticisms made in chapters 2 and 3; but if a significant relation between locus of jural authority and laterality of preference could really be established, this simple association would certainly merit a theoretical investigation. In other words, I think Homans and Schneider's argument as it stands is wrong in any case, but the association they claim to have established is interesting.

Recast as a theory exclusively about preferences, it might have another use, viz., as a guide to a highly speculative reconstruction of the evolution of systems of prescriptive alliance. It is conceivable (though to my mind implausible) that systems of asymmetric alliance could have developed everywhere from a matrilateral preference, and a theory which could explain the preference could perhaps suggest the course of development of one stage in the evolution of such systems. But the value of such a theory, in this context, would be merely suggestive. Though I should never deny the interest or underrate the possible value of such speculation, it has to be admitted that this suggestion is, practically speaking, untestable.

These points are, I think, the most that can be conceded to Homans and Schneider's theory. I conclude that as it stands it is totally erroneous in its application to systems of prescriptive alliance; and, more particularly, that it is irrelevant in the main to the argument of *Les Structures élémentaires de la Parenté*. Preferences, to which alone their theory may have any effective application, constitute an entirely distinct sociological problem, and Lévi-Strauss's argument does not apply to them. Furthermore, on formal and general empirical grounds, as well as in the light of certain particular cases examined (Karadjeri, Yaruro, Siuai, Sherente), I consider that Homans and Schneider also fail to explain preferences.

They conclude with the ambitious claim: "we do not argue that Lévi-Strauss's final cause theory is right or that it is wrong, but only that it is now unnecessary."[44] But they have not only failed to understand what Lévi-Strauss's theory really is, they have neglected to acquire an adequate knowledge of the type of society to which it applies. I have tried to show here that by

[44] P. 59.

125

contrast Lévi-Strauss's argument is not only essentially correct, but uniquely enlightening in its consequences. That is, it helps us to understand what we are trying to understand, viz., the rationale of matrilateral prescriptive alliance, and why the patrilateral system does not exist.

That Homans and Schneider so fail to appreciate Lévi-Strauss's work is due, I think, more than anything else to their psychological preoccupation and theoretical bias. But I should like to affirm categorically that my rejection of their theory is not in any way due to an anti-psychological structuralist dogmatism, but to respect for facts, intensively apprehended, and a simple desire to understand them. I do not care to what academically distinct discipline a proposition, mode of interpretation, or analytical device formally belongs, just so long as it helps us to make sense of social phenomena. This is best achieved, I have maintained here, by the resolution of particular problems; and it is by its degree of success in doing this that we must judge any method of explanation.[45] By this test, in not one case or respect that I have been able to discover has psychology afforded in itself a satisfying or acceptable answer to a sociological problem.[46] It is from this pragmatic base that I have set out to expose the fallaciousness of the psychological explanation of unilateral cross-cousin marriage proposed by Homans and Schneider. It may well be objected that theirs is an inept application of psychological notions and that other psychological interpretations would do better, or that psychological explanations may be illuminating in the analysis of other sociological problems—but one thing at a time. The present case is yet another demonstration of the force of Durkheim's contention: "Whenever a social phenomenon is directly explained by a psychological phenomenon, we may be sure that the explanation is false."[47]

[45] Cf. "I hold myself to be an 'ultimate psychological reductionist,' but I cannot know that I am right so long as the reduction has not been carried out" (Homans, 1958, p. 597).

[46] This is not to say, however, that psychological considerations are never of interest in relation to problems in social anthropology (cf. Leach, 1958b), still less to deny the intrinsic importance or the fascination of psychology.

[47] Durkheim, 1901, p. 128.

BIBLIOGRAPHY

BURLING, ROBBINS

1960 "Garo Avuncular Authority and Matrilateral Cross-Cousin Marriage." *American Anthropologist,* LVIII, 743–49.

DAS, TARAK CHANDRA

1945 *The Purums: An Old Kuki Tribe of Manipur.* Calcutta.

DEACON, A. BERNARD (ed. CAMILLA H. WEDGEWOOD)

1929 "Notes on Some Islands of the New Hebrides." *Journal of the Royal Anthropological Institute,* LVIX, 461–515.

DURKHEIM, ÉMILE

1901 *Les Règles de la méthode sociologique.* (2d ed.) Paris.

EGGAN, FRED

1956 Review of Homans and Schneider, 1955. *American Sociological Review,* XXI, 402–3.

ELKIN, A. P.

1932 "Social Organisation in the Kimberley Division, Northwestern Australia." *Oceania,* II (1931–32), 296–333.

EMMET, DOROTHY

1958 *Function, Purpose, and Powers: Some Concepts in the Study of Individuals and Societies.* London.

EVANS-PRITCHARD, E. E.

1929 "The Study of Kinship in Primitive Societies." *Man,* XXIX, 190–94.

FREEDMAN, MAURICE

1957 Review of Homans and Schneider, 1955. *British Journal of Sociology,* VIII, 285–86.

GLUCKMAN, MAX

1956 Review of Homans and Schneider, 1955. *Man,* LVI, 159.

Goody, Jack

1959 "The Mother's Brother and the Sister's Son in West Africa." *Journal of the Royal Anthropological Institute,* LXXXIX, 61–88.

Hertz, Robert

1909 "La prééminence de la main droite: Étude sur la polarité religieuse." *Revue philosophique,* LXVIII, 553–80. (Also in English translation by Rodney and Claudia Needham, in *Death and The Right Hand,* London, 1960.)

Heusch, Luc de

1958 *Essais sur le symbolisme de l'inceste royal en Afrique.* Brussels.

Hocart, A. M.

1933 *The Progress of Man.* London.

1937 "Kinship Systems." *Anthropos,* XXXII, 345–51. (Reprinted in *The Life-giving Myth,* London, 1952.)

Holmberg, Allan R.

1950 *Nomads of the Long Bow: The Sirionó of Eastern Bolivia.* (Smithsonian Institution, Institute of Social Anthropology, Publication No. 10.) Washington.

Homans, George Caspar

1942 *English Villagers of the Thirteenth Century.* Cambridge, Mass.

1947 "A Conceptual Scheme for the Study of Social Organization." *American Sociological Review,* XII, 13–26.

1951 *The Human Group.* London.

1955 Review of de Josselin de Jong, 1952. *American Anthropologist,* LVII, 136–37.

1958 "Social Behavior as Exchange." *American Journal of Sociology,* LXIII, 597–606.

Homans, George C., and Schneider, David M.

1955 *Marriage, Authority, and Final Causes: A Study of Unilateral Cross-Cousin Marriage.* Glencoe, Ill.

Honigmann, John J.

1959 *The World of Man.* New York.

Josselin de Jong, J. P. B. de

1952 *Lévi-Strauss's Theory on Kinship and Marriage.* (Mededelingen van het Rijksmuseum voor Volkenkunde, No. 10.) Leiden.

KEUNING, JOHANNES

1948 *Verwantschapsrecht en Volksordening, Huwelijksrecht en Erfrecht in het Koeriagebied van Tapanoeli.* Leiden.

KROEBER, A. L.

1927 "Disposal of the Dead." *American Anthropologist,* XXIX, 308–15.

LAGUNA, FREDERICA DE

1952 "Some Dynamic Forces in Tlingit Society." *Southwestern Journal of Anthropology,* VIII, 1–12.

LEACH, E. R.

1950 Review of Murdock, 1949. *Man,* L, 107–8.

1951 "The Structural Implications of Matrilateral Cross-Cousin Marriage." *Journal of the Royal Anthropological Institute,* LXXXI, 23–55.

1958a "Concerning Trobriand Clans and the Kinship Category 'Tabu.'" *Cambridge Papers in Social Anthropology,* No. 1, pp. 120–45.

1958b "Magical Hair." *Journal of the Royal Anthropological Institute,* LXXXVIII, 147–64.

LÉVI-STRAUSS, CLAUDE

1949 *Les Structures élémentaires de la Parenté.* Paris.

1958 *Anthropologie structurale.* Paris.

LOWIE, ROBERT H.

1956 Review of Homans and Schneider, 1955. *American Anthropologist,* LVIII, 1144.

McCONNEL, URSULA H.

1939–40 "Social Organisation of the Tribes of Cape York Peninsula, North Queensland." *Oceania,* X, 54–72, 434–55.

MALINOWSKI, BRONISLAW

1929 *The Sexual Life of Savages in Northwestern Melanesia.* London.

MAUSS, MARCEL

1920 "L'Extension du potlatch en Mélanésie." *Anthropologie,* XXX, 396–97.

1925 "Essai sur le Don: Forme et raison de l'échange dans les sociétés archaïques." *Année sociologique,* N.S. I (1923–24), 30–186. Paris. (Also in English translation, by IAN CUNNISON, as *The Gift,* London, 1954.)

MAYBURY-LEWIS, D. H. P.

1958 "Kinship and Social Organisation in Central Brazil." *Proceedings of the 32nd International Congress of Americanists*, pp. 123–35. Copenhagen.

1960 "Parallel Descent and the Apinayé Anomaly." *Southwestern Journal of Anthropology*, XVI, 191–216.

MITCHELL, G. DUNCAN

1959 *Sociology: The Study of Social Systems.* London.

MURDOCK, GEORGE PETER

1934*a* "Kinship and Social Behavior among the Haida." *American Anthropologist*, XXXVI, 355–85.

1934*b* *Our Primitive Contemporaries.* New York.

1949 *Social Structure.* New York.

1957 "World Ethnographic Sample." *American Anthropologist*, LIX, 664–87.

1959 *Africa: Its Peoples and Their Culture History.* New York.

NEEDHAM, RODNEY

1956 Review of Homans and Schneider, 1955. *American Journal of Sociology*, LXII, 107–8.

1958*a* "A Structural Analysis of Purum Society." *American Anthropologist*, LX, 75–101.

1958*b* "The Formal Analysis of Prescriptive Patrilateral Cross-Cousin Marriage." *Southwestern Journal of Anthropology*, XIV, 199–219.

1960*a* "Chawte Social Structure." *American Anthropologist*, LXII, 236–53.

1960*b* "Structure and Change in Asymmetric Alliance." *American Anthropologist*, LXII, 499–503.

1960*c* "Alliance and Classification among the Lamet." *Sociologus*, X, 97–119.

1960*d* "The Left Hand of the Mugwe: An Analytical Note on the Structure of Meru Symbolism." *Africa*, XXX, 20–33.

1961 "An Analytical Note on the Structure of Sirionó Society." *Southwestern Journal of Anthropology*, XVIII, 239–55.

NIMUENDAJÚ, CURT (trans. ROBERT H. LOWIE)

1942 *The Šerente.* (Publications of the Frederick Webb Hodge Anniversary Publication Fund, Vol. IV.) Los Angeles.

Oliver, Douglas L.

1955 *A Solomon Island Society: Kinship and Leadership among the Siuai of Bougainville.* Cambridge, Mass.

Petrullo, Vincenzo

1939 "The Yaruro of the Capanarapo River, Venezuela." *Bulletin of the Bureau of American Ethnology,* CXXIII, 161–290. Washington.

Radcliffe-Brown, A. R.

1924 "The Mother's Brother in South Africa." *South African Journal of Science,* XXI, 542–55. (Reprinted in Radcliffe-Brown, 1952, pp. 15–31.)

1952 *Structure and Function in Primitive Society.* London.

Schapera, I.

1957 "Marriage of Near Kin among the Tswana." *Africa,* XXVII, 139–60.

Slater, M. K.

1959 "Ecological Factors in the Origin of Incest." *American Anthropologist,* LXI, 1042–59.

Smith, Edwin W., and Dale, Andrew Murray

1920 *The Ila-speaking Peoples of Northern Rhodesia.* 2 vols. London.

Thomson, Donald F.

1935 "The Joking Relationship and Organized Obscenity in North Queensland." *American Anthropologist,* XXXVII, 460–90.

Toulmin, Stephen

1953 *The Philosophy of Science: An Introduction.* London.

Vroklage, B. A. G.

1952–53 *Ethnographie der Belu in Zentral-Timor.* 3 vols. Leiden.

Waissmann, F.

1959 "The Decline and Fall of Causality." In A. C. Crombie (ed.), *Turning Points in Physics.* Amsterdam, 1959.

Wouden, F. A. E. van

1956 "Locale groepen en dubbele afstamming in Kodi, West Soemba." *Bijdragen tot de Taal-, Land- en Volkenkunde,* CXII, 204–46.

INDEX